For la belle Tahir

THE STREETS OF EAST LONDON

with warm regards from
her "amused" tutor,

William J. Fishman

26/iv/1990

THE STREETS OF EAST LONDON

William J. Fishman

with photographs by
Nicholas Breach

DUCKWORTH

Seventh impression 1989
Sixth impression 1987
Fifth impression 1985
Fourth impression 1983
Third impression 1981
Second impression 1980
First published in 1979 by
Gerald Duckworth & Co. Ltd.
The Old Piano Factory
43 Gloucester Crescent,
London NW1

Designed by Patrick Leeson

ISBN 0 7156 1391 X cased
ISBN 0 7156 1416 9 paper

British Library Cataloguing in Publication Data

Fishman, William Jack
    The streets of East London.
    1. London. East End—History
    I. Title
    II. Breach, Nicolas
    942.1´5   DA685.E1

    ISBN 0-7156-1416-9

Filmset and printed in Great Britain by
BAS Printers Limited, Over Wallop, Hampshire

CONTENTS

Frontispiece On the corner of Brick Lane and Cheshire Street

Chestnut seller, Cobb Street

PREFACE

The East End of London, to this day, has a uniqueness of character which transcends period and generation. We have attempted to isolate this by submitting some impressionistic views in picture and text of, albeit, a limited sector of our area—past and present. We have been less concerned with generalities than with specifics, which, in our reckoning, capture the unchanging essence of East End life.

During our continual excursions into the streets, we found our investigations and rewards growing like Topsy. We were forced, therefore, to limit our scope, geographically, to Whitechapel ('The East End in the East End', according to writer J. H. Mackay) and its adjacent bounds, and our comparative time spans to between, say, the late Victorian and Edwardian and post-1945 eras. It could be argued, and rightly so, that Bethnal Green, Poplar and the Docks are traditionally part of the East End scene, and that their exclusion is unjustified. Also, the inter-war years have only been briefly mentioned. All areas and periods need a study of their own, and, in our view, their absence does not detract from the aim of our enterprise, which is to capture the nature and character of East End life, to transmit these to our readers, and, perhaps, to inculcate in them a desire to go and seek further. For Tower Hamlets is a historical, social and literary treasure house, and we have merely revealed a glimpse of its potential.

We hereby acknowledge, with gratitude, the following individuals and institutions who have helped us on our way: Tower Hamlets Borough Council, particularly its leader Councillor Paul Beas-ley, under whom potent forces are being mobilised to attract new industries to the area, including a plan to alter dramatically the face of Dockland into an attractive housing and parkland area; Martin Cresswell and Stephen Carey, also of the Council; Tower Hamlets Public Library, especially its librarian-historian, Bernard Nurse, whose practical aid on sources and illustrations was invaluable. Likewise Commissioner Mrs Hannam, Captains Rea and Warren of the Salvation Army; Caroline Adams, Youth and Community Worker with the Spitalfields Bengali community; Archbishop Trevor Huddleston; Donald Rumbelow of the City Police; Terry McCarthy, curator of the National Museum of Labour History; Raphael Samuel, historian; Sid Bloom, proprietor of *Bloom's*.

For the means and opportunities for carrying out this project we are indebted to Trevor Smith, Head of the Department of Political Studies at Queen Mary College, Mr Barnett Shine of the Barnett Shine Educational Foundation, and Mrs Valerie Greenberg for her impeccable work on the typescript and her highly professional advice on syntax.

Last, but not least, our thanks to those who kindly sent us photos for illustrations and to the citizens of East London and beyond, who appear here, voluntarily or involuntarily, and thereby made this book possible.

All the undated photographs are by Nicholas Breach and were taken specially for the book.

W. J. F.
N. B.

THE STREETS OF EAST LONDON

So how can you tell me you're lonely
Say for you the sun don't shine.
Let me take you by the hand
And lead you through the streets of London
I will show you something
That will make you change your mind.

(*Ralph McTell, Top pop song, 'Reprise Records' 1974*)

Arthur Morrison, not an unperceptive oberver of East End life, essayed in 'A street' (1891)* to generalise from the particular by his judgment on *one* street, which, for him, typified *all* in East London:

> Where in the East End lies this street? Everywhere . . . This street of the square holes is hundreds of miles long. That it is planned in short lengths is true, but there is no other way in the world that can more properly be called a single street, because of its dismal lack of accent, its sordid uniformity, its utter remoteness from delight.

He was quite wrong.

Not only did 'the long and mighty tangled chain' of 'tortuous maze' offer a variety of conflicting architecture. There was also a host of diverse communities, segregated and self-identified according to street, alley, ethnic root, religion, occupation (often unlawful), fixed urbanite or immigrant countryman—a patchwork quilt of settlements with interwoven subcultures.

Walk the streets of East London today and yesterday and you will have rubbed shoulders with Irish cockneys, Russo-Polish Jews, Chinese, Somalis, West Africans, Indians and white Anglo-Saxon Protestants, the coloured minorities always ensconced in their sharply defined ghettos.

*All references are to the Bibliography, p. 132 below.

There are permanencies which defy generations. Life, from time immemorial, is tough; labour hard and monotonous. People work to live, not vice versa, a postscript to the past with its daily struggle for bread. The weekend is sacrosanct, as it was purported to be more than a century ago—but not for churchgoing. It is a time for fun, for a collective escape to the updated gin-palace-cum-penny-gaff, that is, into the glittering vulgarity of the 'local', now enhanced by the fleshly gyrations of 'strippers'; or, for the less adventurous, to the tribal gathering and ritual chants of the Bingo Hall. Bank holidays bring extended relief: yesterday by way of a trip by 'Shanks's pony' (on foot) or rail to the 'Flats' or Epping Forest or boozy street parties aboard the pleasure steamer cruising gently along the banks of the Thames; today by diesel train or family car to Southend—still our Whitechapel-by-the-Sea! The Yiddish theatre is gone. But the Bangla-Deshi cinema in Brick Lane is full to capacity, sustaining the culture of the stranger.

Specifics, not generalities, depict the uniqueness of East End life. (Petticoat Lane is a false frontier with its Sunday transformation into a cosmopolis!) Bordering the commercial centre and the river, its destiny was prescribed. It has always attracted the transient and the feckless. Its settled citizens have always serviced the City and the docks. It was, and still is, in the jargon, almost one hundred per cent proletarian.

Images caught by our camera will, we hope, emphasise the nuances of working-class activity set against the background of local streets. Streets without people constitute a void. In the East End they combine to produce a marvellously colourful whole. Look at the faces of the costers and the customers that throng

Porters in Spitalfields Market, early morning

Cheshire Street, Club Row, Wentworth Street and the Whitechapel Waste markets. Clusters of musing bovines, touchingly curious but aggressive youngsters, some splendid gargoyles, merge effortlessly. It is in the nature of the place that the unfamiliar and the eccentric are still an integral part of the East End phenomenon.

Continuity is there: in the few surviving rumps of street communities, in the markets, in the pubs, in the handful of leprous, urine-soaked courtyards and alleys, in the odd 'Good pull-up for carmen', in the Hebrew insignia on decaying façades of the last remaining synagogues. But a crime has been committed against the past. In the race for functional conformity, and from the pressing needs for rehousing the people, the little streets and their ancient

Locals at Cheshire Street market

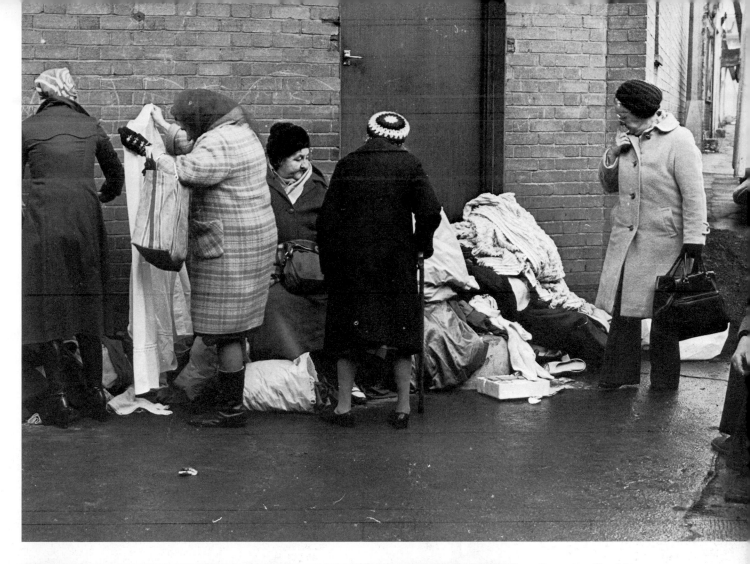

Buyers at Cheshire
Street market

Butcher's shop,
Watney Street, *c.* 1910

11

Along the Whitechapel Waste

In Wentworth Street

Derelict backs and tower block, Stepney

communities have fallen before the demolishers—a development now recognised, too late, as an error of judgment. Juxtapose the new high-rise Bastilles against the residual one-up-one-down Victorian cottages, and one can sense the loss in human terms. Dirt piles high in the crumbling streets. Why clean up when the bulldozer is on the march? And the wasteland continues to extend itself as the rubble heaps replace the cosy, one-storeyed, back-to-back brick structures, which once nurtured the same families for generations.

Even so, the past is as inexorable as the present. The streets of East London make it so. From Spitalfields to Limehouse, three, albeit spiritually inoperative, Hawksmoor churches—Christ Church, Spitalfields; St. George's-in-the-East, Highway; St. Anne's, Limehouse—still cut the skyline, while from Brick Lane to Cephas Avenue, Mile End, three ancient breweries, in contrast—Truman, Hanbury and Bux-

ton, Brick Lane; Watney Mann, along the White-chapel Road; Bass Charrington, in the Mile End Road—still flourish, sustained over the centuries by popular demand. The great stores, Wickhams and Gardiners, once landmarks, have vanished, while the stalls muster weekly, as of yore, along the Whitechapel and Mile End roads, offering a wide range of cheap, up-to-date consumer items to the crowds of local bargain hunters. Astride those thronging the Mile End Waste lie the symbols of perpetuity—the 'holy' stone commemorating the birthplace of the Salvation Army in 1865, sited opposite the ancient gates which open up to Christopher Wren's Trinity House Almshouses, constructed in 1695 for '28 decayed masters and commanders of ships or widows of such'. Homage is duly accorded to a great mariner: across the main thoroughfare on a wall built to enclose a space where once stood No. 88 Mile End Road, a plaque starkly proclaims:

14

Early nineteenth-century cottages, Halcrow Street

On this site
stood a house occupied
for some years by
CAPTAIN JAMES COOK R.N., F.R.S
1728–1779
Circumnavigator and Explorer

A place of change, of innovation? Sheer necessity demanded it. Contrast East End kids today with the 'bootless nippers' of yesterday. Had not Doctor Barnardo focused on the issue of child care? Social welfare prolongs life. Thus did the London Hospital (inaugurated in 1757 on the present site, with 161 beds), by its very inception, inculcate the introduction of private and, later, state-aided institutions concerned with safeguarding public health. Add to these a galaxy of pioneers in kindred schemes, who also found the East End slums conducive to practical experimentation: Canon Barnett with his Toynbee Hall University Settlement (a model for developmental replicas around the world) and sponsor-creator of the free Whitechapel Art Gallery and Library; Annie Besant and the Pankhursts, leading advocates for women's rights, who recruited their rank-and-file militants in Bow and Poplar; Rudolf Rocker, gentile leader of a Yiddish Libertarian group, who, in the Jubilee Street Anarchist Club, helped to expose thousands of Russo-Polish Jewish immigrants to Western culture, and thereby ensured the flowering of diverse talents which might have been lost.

To the curious and the imaginative the streets of East London offer a voyage of discovery into a unique past and present. It is hoped that the following will provide the *hors d'oeuvres* for what could, by a follow-up walk on the ground, become a pleasurable feast.

15

Inside the *Jack the Ripper*

Barmaid, *Jack the Ripper*

Mercers Cottages, Salmon Lane

Artillery Passage, on the bounds of the City

The Frying Pan, Thrawl Street

Early Sunday morning in Cobb Street

Dawn in Brick Lane   Assembly Passage, off the Mile End Road   Wood buildings by Whitechapel Station

Puma Court, where Dickens walked

Spectacle Alley, Whitechapel, *c.* 1915

Christ Church School, Brick Lane

Half Moon Passage, off Alie Street

POVERTY

Ninety years ago a young Anglo-German writer who had taken to walking the streets of Whitechapel saw an 'Empire of Hunger':

> The East End of London is the hell of poverty. Like an enormous, black, motionless, giant kracken, the poverty of London lies there in lurking silence and encircles with its mighty tentacles the life and wealth of the City and of the West End . . . (*Mackay, p. 152*)

Similar observations on this great Wen had previously been voiced by Dickens and Mayhew. Not long before (1883) the outraged priest William C. Preston's horrific revelations in *The Bitter Cry of Outcast London* finally shook the complacency of Victorian London.

London was indeed a City of Dreadful Night (William Morris). A strange race prowled the streets from penny-gaff to gin-palace. In the dimmed back yards came the shrill cries of cock-fighting or 'ratting', the howls of barefisted boxers, whose activities sometimes ended in the morgue: the furtive book-maker ('bookie') calling his illegal bets in some secluded cobbled alleyway, and always the awful wailing shrieks of some woman or child being beaten by a drunken father. And sex, the old escape from sordid reality, offered by its female acolytes patrolling the gas-lit courtways by night, as they sought the male destined to provide them with the wherewithal for a loaf of bread and a 4d. doss in a common lodging house.

Impressionistic accounts convey a common picture of degradation and want. Henrietta Barnett contributes a description of her parish of St. Jude's (Whitechapel) in 1873:

There were two or three narrow streets lined with fairly decent cottages occupied entirely by Jews, but, with these exceptions, the whole parish was covered with a network of courts and alleys. None of these courts had roads. In some the houses were three storeys high and hardly six feet apart, the sanitary accommodation being pits in the cellars; in other courts the houses were lower, wooden and dilapidated, a stand pipe at the end providing the only water. Each chamber was the home of a family who sometimes owned their indescribable furniture, but in most cases the rooms were let out furnished for 8d. a night. In many instances broken windows had been repaired with paper and rags, the bannisters had been used for firewood, and the paper hung from the walls which were the residence of countless vermin . . . If the men worked at all it was as casual dock labourers, enjoying the sense of gambling, which the uncertainty of obtaining work gave. But usually they did not work; they stole or received stolen goods, they hawked, begged, cadged, lived on each other with generous indiscrimination, drank, gambled, fought, and when they became too well known to the police, moved to another neighbourhood.

(*Barnett, vol. 1, pp. 73–4*)

Fourteen years later the scene is unchanged. Against this background Mackay catches the tensions, the bitterness, the suspicion and malevolence felt by the inhabitants towards the well-breeched outsiders. Like Arthur Morrison he, too, had walked with a companion through the labyrinthine courts of the Jago and Brick Lane where 'everywhere . . . the neglect of hunger . . . daily fights a frightful battle with death'. The two strangers make their way down the middle of the street, for to venture on to the sidewalk was to court danger:

A court in Whitechapel, *c.* 1915

Whitechapel workhouse, from Jack London's *People of the Abyss* (1903)

Small doss house, from the same

Sometimes a window was half opened, a bushy head thrust out, and shy, curious eyes followed half in fear, half in hate, the wholly unusual sight of the strangers. A man was hammering at a broken cart which obstructed the whole width of the street. He did not respond to the greetings of the passers-by: stupefied, he stared at them as at an apparition from another world; a woman who had been cowering in a dark corner, motionless, rose terrified, pressed her child with both hands against her breast hardly covered with rags, and propped herself, as if to offer resistance, against the wall, not once taking her eyes off the two men . . .

(*Mackay*)

The worst casualties were the children, after they survived their first handicap—being born. (Jack London recorded: 'in the West End 18% of children die before 5 years of age; in the East End 55% of the children die before 5 years of age . . . Slaughter! Herod did not do quite so badly.' Baby-selling was rife, a casual exchange used as a last resort by a starving

From *Spitalfields Nippers* (1912)

The magistrate accepted the rebuke. No one knew the boy. 'He was without beginning or antecedent, a waif, a stray, a young cub seeking his food in the jungle of empire, preying upon the weak and being preyed upon by the strong.' Certainly so, but much worse were the prospects facing a young girl—for the 'crime' of being born female.

> Man to Man so oft unjust
> Is always so to Woman.

In the predatory climate engendered by 'laissez-faire', women were the most vulnerable. For those categorised by Charles Booth as on or below the poverty line, it was an unrewarding struggle for life. As a child she would be 'mother' to a large, ever-increasing brood, should her own be out charring or 'taking out laundry' to augment her man's meagre income (if he was not already unemployed!). At the lowest level she faced continual hazards: an incestuous attack by father or brother, a beating by a drunken parent, perhaps only relieved by taking to the streets. The afflictions of labour bore heaviest on East End women. Innocence was short-lived, demoralisation inevitable. Here the record of man's inhumanity to woman is most blatant.

Margaret Harkness (1889) observing a group of girls applying for work in a local factory notes:

> A more miserable set of girls it would be difficult to find anywhere. They had only just escaped from Board School, but many of them had faces wise with wickedness, and eyes out of which all traces of maidenhood had vanished; the 'universal adjective' fell from their lips as a term of endearment, whilst the foulest names were given to girls they did not like, also blows and kisses by way of emphasis.
>
> (*Law (1), pp. 103–9*)

They are offered work at 5d. a day, 'enough to buy bread with'. As new recruits to the vast reservoir of labour, they had no alternative but to accept. 'It's no good to talk to the girls about combination, they're so downtrodden and mean-spirited . . . They [the capitalists] use the girls to cut the throats of the men . . . It's work, work, work, with them from the time they get up till they go to bed, except on Sundays.' Yet mutual aid, the poor helping the poor in adversity, was never absent. 'They're good to one another, they are. You'd be surprised to see what they'll do to help a girl

mother or to satisfy the immediate needs of a habitual drunkard. Cruelty and insensitivity infected the young. Mackay was shocked by a group of children 'amusing themselves by the sight of the dying fits of a cat whose eyes they had gouged out, and whom they had hanged by the tail. When the bleeding, tortured animal jerked with its feet to get away, they struck at it with the cruel awful pleasure children take in visible pain'. Begging and thieving in some parishes were, not surprisingly, the norm. London posed the dilemma in the case of a young delinquent tried for stealing:

> Fresh in my mind is the picture of a boy in the dock of an East End police court. His head was barely visible above the railing. He was being proved guilty of stealing two shillings from a woman, which he had spent, not for candy and cakes and a good time, but for food.
> 'Why didn't you ask the woman for food?' the magistrate demanded, in a hurt sort of tone. 'She would surely have given you something to eat.'
> 'If I 'ad arsked 'er, I'd got locked up for begging' was the boy's reply.
>
> (*London*)

Assembling matchboxes at 2½d. per gross, Bethnal Green, *c.* 1900

that's ill, and how they'll put themselves about to buy crape when a girl is dead and has to be buried.' The suffering of a lifetime could be compensated by the prospect of a 'correct' burial. For the poor, the ultimate horror went beyond dying. It was the threat of a pauper's grave which, in its cold anonymity, evidenced society's final rejection of their human identity. Harkness recalls an old woman who only accepts alms to ensure that her dying daughter 'met the Almighty like a lady. "I've got her a muslin dress, in which she made her first communion, to lay her out in. I'd like to think as she'd stand before the Almighty in a pair of white silk stockings!"'

The degradation of women was concomitant with an oppressive society. Respectable Victorians were shocked at the widespread incidence of women employed in slave labour. Match-making provided a domestic industry with a legacy of long-term exploitation. Preston, among his revelations, finds that one woman 'with a crippled hand, maintains herself and a blind husband by matchbox making, for which she is remunerated [at] . . . 2¼d. a gross', out of which she has to pay a girl 1d. a gross to help (*Preston, p. 10*). A description of a homeworker is given form and poignancy by Harkness. In a dark, low attic room a woman lives alone with three small children. A fourth, a lame girl, lies asleep with her crutches resting against the bundle of rags which serve as a pillow.

. . . the woman's hands were busy with the matchboxes. Strips of magenta paper and thin pieces of wood came together with the help of a paste brush. They were then thrown on the ground to dry, forming pyramids of trays and lids which would presently be made into matchboxes, tied up with string and sent back to factories which give 2¼d. per gross for matchboxes. Two little children stood on the floor amidst the trays and lids and an older boy chopped wood in a corner of the room with a look on his face of hungry impatience . . . The room had no furniture but the table, the bed, and a few old hampers; a heap of coke was near the fireplace with which to dry the woman's work, also some cabbage leaves and onion stalks. This refuse the children would eat later if nothing else was forthcoming. It had been thrown in as fuel by the vendor of the coke, and a dog would scarcely have swallowed it. *But in these days animals are better off than slum children.* (The owner of that attic has been heard to say: 'My dog turns tail when I go in; it's so disgusting.')

Thirteen years later (1903), long after the successful match girls' strike, Jack London asks his reader to—

Mrs Robinson of Bethnal Green stuffing mattresses for 1/- an hour, *c.* 1900

Conceive of an old woman, broken and dying, supporting herself and four children, and paying three shillings per week rent, by making match boxes at 2¼d. per gross. Twelve dozen boxes for 2¼d., and, in addition, finding her own paste and thread! She never knew a day off, either for sickness, rest or recreation. Each day and every day, Sundays as well, she toiled fourteen hours. Her day's stint was seven gross, for which she received 1s. 3¾d. In the week of 98 hours' work she made 7,066 matchboxes, and earned 4/10¼d. less paste and thread.

(*London, p. 209*)

Why this infliction on the 'woman of the lower Ghetto classes [who] is as much the slave of her husband as is the Indian squaw . . .'? London notes:

Home industry: making brushes, *c.* 1900

The men are economically dependent on their masters, and the women are economically dependent on the men. The result is the woman gets the beating the man should give to his master, and she can do nothing. There are the kiddies, and he is the breadwinner, and she dare not send him to jail and leave herself and children to starve. Evidence to convict can rarely be obtained when such cases come into the courts; as a rule the trampled wife and mother is weeping and hysterically beseeching the magistrate to let her husband off for the kiddies' sake.

Prostitution, for the young girl, offered one way out, although relief proved ephemeral. 'The profession of a prostitute is the only career in which the maximum income is paid to the newest apprentice' (*Booth, W., p. 51*). Harkness reiterated that the overwhelming pressure was the need for food. 'Virtue is easy enough when a woman has plenty to eat, and a character to keep, but it's quite different when a girl is starving.' Many an East End lass got the message. The streets provided a world free from the immediacy of want and drudgery as well as the prospects of wealth and comfort. At the least they could expect to make more in one night than a whole week at the sweatshop. The girl who recognised her own physical talents could exploit them to the full by way of the glittering thoroughfares of the West End. But the liberation of the streets was an illusion. The cost would soon be exacted, for the penalties of disease and degradation were inescapable.

Much of this presupposes that, even in poverty, most East Enders could claim a permanent roof over their heads. This was not so. By the 1880s the East End was already an over-congested ghetto of displaced labour, where housing was at a premium. Why?

In 1860 Britain was at the peak of her industrial hegemony, which had led to a dramatic polarisation into two main classes—a 'rich becoming richer, and a poor, poorer'. In London this was reflected in the contrasts in domestic housing. Splendid town houses for the wealthy merchant, noble or country landlord sprang up from the City through to Mayfair; and from the Bank to Hammersmith one could walk through street after street of fashionable stately mansions in clean, tree-lined quasi-boulevards, picturesquely lit at night by gaslight.

For this and for the construction of new central railway termini, schools and offices, it was necessary to demolish the oldest, and most vulnerable areas, that is, those inhabited by the casual and labouring poor. Earliest to go was Dickens's famous St. Giles, a hive of broken-down hovels, gin shops, professional *lumpen*—thieves, pimps and prostitutes—such that no Peeler dare enter there alone; but also the only homes of those artisans and labourers who serviced the West End. The dispossessed fled eastward, seeking their own kind and to continue their lives in the old style. There followed the destruction of similar areas north and east of the City, the commercial centre eager to expand its own institutional frontiers. The process was aided by Disraeli's Artisans Dwellings Act of 1875, ostensibly a piece of progressive legislation to replace the slums by sanitary and functional accommodation for the 'lower' classes. But replacement housing remained in short supply, partly due to the unavoidable time lag between demolition and reconstruction. Meanwhile the exodus developed its own momentum, filling up in turn the already overcrowded East End, which had not only housed itinerant City-employed artisans and workers and seamen and ships' craftsmen of the docks, but had always served as an entrepôt for new immigrants.

In 1902 Jack London could still discern that the 'poor quarters of the City proper are constantly being destroyed and the main stream of the unhoused is towards the east'. The result was labour competing for accommodation so that for landlords 'the houses of the poor [became] greater profit earners than the mansions of the rich'. Even the hasty addition of cheap, jerry-built, back-to-back cottages in any available space failed to meet demand. Hence the expansion of lodging houses, or temporary 'doss' houses, which added an even less salubrious dimension to the image of East London.

The most horrific conditions were attributed to doss houses catering for the casual poor. At their best they were merely free of criminals, prostitutes and vermin. But the majority, located in Spitalfields, St. George's and in the dock parishes, were not. Margaret Harkness, who visited a number during the 1880s, describes a typical cheap 'doss' priced at 4d. single for the night. A gloomy, decaying, two-storeyed house is divided into 'dormitories', i.e. rooms 'full of small iron bedsteads covered with a grey blanket. They were arranged in two rows against the walls, and were so close together that it was impossible to move between them . . .' Downstairs in the main kitchen, while a gambling session was in full play—

> Men and women stood cooking their supper; emptying into tins and saucepans bits of meat, scraps of bread and cold potatoes they had begged, stolen or picked up during the day. Hungry children held plates ready for the savoury messes, and received blows and kicks from their parents when they came too near the fire, or interfered with the cooking arrangements.
>
> Crouching on the floor, gnawing a bone, was a hungry man. His face was sodden with drink. He had swollen features, palsied hands, and trembling feet. He had probably begun life in this Christian country as a homeless boy in the streets and most likely will close his days in the casual ward of some workhouse. Then
>
> > 'Rattle his bones over the stones
> > He's only a pauper, who nobody owns!'
>
> The lodgers threw him scraps, and laughed to see him tearing his food to pieces, devouring it like a dog on the ground.
>
> (*Law (2), pp. 108–11*)

This probably exemplified a more respectable establishment. Others served as a rendezvous for the underground—thieves' kitchens, where only the Salvationist slum lassie could enter without fear and no policeman dared to venture alone. 'A clergyman found his way in one Sunday evening. He was stripped, in order that the men might see if he was a detective. Finding all his linen marked with the same name and nothing in his pockets, they kicked him out, advising him never to come there again unless he was plentifully supplied with soup tickets.' (*Law (2)*)

The competition among the labouring poor for

Andrew Johnson, old East Ender, by the Booth memorial

scarce permanent accommodation created an army of house sweaters who operated on the basis of 'not only are houses to let but . . . sub-let down to the very room'. Everywhere there were notices 'a part of a room to let' where beds were occupied on a three-relay system, twenty-four hours a day, i.e. three tenants in each bed so that it never grew cold. Likewise the floor beneath could be profitably utilised.

Rent was a yoke which bore heavily on workmen. Jack London estimated that:

> Nearly 50% of the workers pay from one quarter to a half of their earnings in rent. The average rent for the larger part of the East End is from 4/- to 6/- per week for one room, while skilled mechanics earning 35/- per week are forced to part with 15/- of it for two or three pokey little dens, in which they strive desperately to obtain some semblance of home life. *And rents are going up all the time.* In one street in Stepney the increase in only two years has been from 13/- to 18/-; in another street from 11/- to 15/-; whilst in Whitechapel, two room houses that recently rented for 10/- are now costing 21/- . . . When land is worth £20,000 to £30,000 an acre, someone must pay the landlord.

> *(London)*

The hazards resulting from non-payment of rent by an honest worker fallen sick are cited by William Booth in a case illustrating how the 'Army of Despair' is never short of recruits:

> Mr. T., Margaret Place, Gascoigne Place, Bethnal Green, is a bootmaker by trade. He is a good hand, and has earned three shillings and sixpence to four shillings and sixpence a day. He and his wife were taken ill last Christmas, and went to the London Hospital; they were there three months. Directly after they had been taken ill, their furniture was seized for three weeks' rent which was owing. Consequently on becoming convalescent they were homeless. They came out about the same time. He went out to a lodging house for a night or two, until she came out. He then had twopence, and she had sixpence which a nurse had given her. They went to a lodging house together, but the society there was dreadful. Next day he had a day's work, and got two shillings and sixpence and on the strength of this they took a furnished room at tenpence per day (payable nightly). His work lasted a few weeks, when he was again taken ill, lost his job, and spent all his money. He pawned a shirt and apron for a shilling and spent that too . . . He is now minus tools and cannot work at his own job, and does anything he can. They spent their last twopence on a pen'orth each of tea and sugar. In two days they had a slice of bread and butter each, that's all. They are both very weak through want of food.

> *(Booth, W., pp. 42–3)*

For the homeless there were two alternatives for survival: the Salvation Army hostel or—the ultimate humiliation, conferred on both genuine unemployed and pauper alike—the hated Bastille, the workhouse. A foretaste was the casual ward, where they could find temporary respite. In times of depression, as the queues outside lengthened one could hear the melancholy refrains, rendered in unison, of:

> What will become of us,
> If things go on this way,
> If honest working-men
> Are starving day by day.

or 'Starving in the Queen's Highway'.

The casuals were interviewed one by one by the master, and subjected to the most degrading questioning. If accepted, they must first submit themselves to washing naked in a communal bath. In *Out of Work* Harkness (under her pseudonym of Law) describes what happens to an unemployed worker, Jo:

Salvation Army 'Farthing Breakfasts', Hanbury Street, 1880

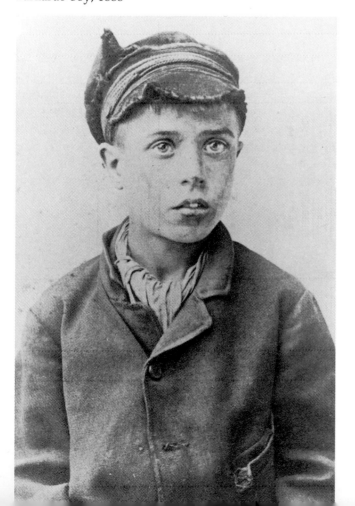

Barnardo boy, 1888

He was . . . taken into a cell that measured eight feet by four feet, at the end of which was a small dark hole called the stone pit.

The cell was lighted by a jet of gas, and the first thing he saw was an inscription, written in large uncouth letters on the white-washed wall opposite the entrance:

*I've served my Queen and my country for 15 years
and this is what I've come to.*

. . . the cell had no furniture whatsoever, except the mattress and the rug on which he was sitting. An icy wind swept through the stone pit, so he went to see if a door would shut off the draught. But no door was there, only a large iron window, with bars across, through which flints must be thrown when broken, into a yard beneath. The wind blew in gusts through the iron bars, and he shivered, for the warm bath made him feel the cold air creeping about his chilly limbs, under his clothes, through his skin to his flesh.

Breaking stones was compulsory for casuals in return for 'food and lodging'. A hammer and large blocks of granite lay in the pit. There was no seat, and the floor of the place dipped in the middle, so it was difficult to stand upright. Work began in the morning.

37

Meanwhile the overseer brought his meal for the night, 'a small tin of gruel and a small piece of bread (the whole provision could have been put into a tea cup)'. To meet his keep he was forced to stay two days and three nights, for he was unable to crush the granite. ('It required a knack!') The task seemed deliberately geared to induce misery and demoralisation:

> Three times a day he received his rations of gruel and bread. At night he stopped work when the gas was extinguished; the rest of the time he stood, or sat in the stone pit, trying to find the knack. The stones would not split up small enough to pass through the iron grating, they either shattered into atoms, or lay on the ground in oblong nobs that no hammer would crack. The stone pit sloped into a hole in the middle. So he found it difficult not to slip when standing up, and impossible to throw stones through the grating when sitting down. Besides, the place was dark, and the damp cold air there made him shiver.

In one way it was a blessed release when a small piece of granite flew into his eye. The master was forced to let him out with the warning, 'Don't come back here within the month. If you do, you'll be kept in twice the time, remember, but if you come, we'll put you to pick oakum, you're not good for anything else'. (*Law (2), pp. 181–6*.) No wonder that, for the destitute, prison was far more congenial than a stint in the casual.

The old, the lame, the blind and the beggar faced alike the terrifying reality of the workhouse—for the poor the most feared and hated of institutions. Such attitudes are self-evident as we read a contemporary description of the Whitechapel workhouse, a model of its kind, recalling the clinical inhumanity of a Nazi labour camp.

> Ringing the workhouse bell, they enter into a forecourt of neat flower beds, closely shaven grass plots, smooth paths, and trees which had been pruned until their branches had reached the *legitimate* amount of foliage. The Bastille stretched further than the eye could see, and seemed a standing rebuke to its poverty-stricken surroundings, for it was clean . . . not a spot on it, not a stain, nothing to show a trace of sympathy with the misery and sin of the people who lived in this neighbourhood.

> The Whitechapel Union is a model workhouse; that is to say it is the Poor Law incarnate in stone and brick. The men are not allowed to smoke in it, not even when they are in their dotage; the young women never taste tea, and the old ones may not indulge in a cup during the long afternoons, only at half past six o'clock morning and night, when they receive a small hunk of bread with butter scraped over the surface, and a mug of neat beverage which is so dear to their hearts as well as their stomachs. The young people never go out, never see a visitor, and the old only get one holiday in the month. Then the aged paupers may be seen skipping like lambkins outside the doors of the Bastille while they jabber to their friends and relatives. A little gruel morning and night, meat twice a week, that is the food of grown-up people, seasoned with hard work and prison discipline. Doubtless this Bastille offers no premium to idle and improvident habits, but what shall we say of the woman, or man, maimed by misfortune, who must come there or die in the street?

The master was proud to report that *his* house was run on Samuel Smiles's precepts of self-help. 'We grind our own corn, we make our own clothes, boots and coffins; in fact meat, grain and clothes stuff are all that we take from the outside public.' This was borne out by a visit to the labour rooms, where the able-bodied worked on their dull, monotonous tasks without respite.

> Tailors squatted on tables, bootmakers cobbled and patched, men plaited mats; each pauper had his task, and each knew that the morrow would bring the same work, that as surely as the sun rises and sets, his task would be the same tomorrow as it was at that moment. Six o'clock would set him free for tea, but after that he would be handed over to an instructor until bed-time.

> The Whitechapel Union allows no man to remain idle from the time he gets up until he goes to bed again. A sodden look had settled on the faces of the older men and they apparently thought little of what they were doing . . . not a voice was to be heard in the workshops, the men did not whistle or sing; They looked like schoolboys in disgrace rather than free-born English citizens.

> (*Law (1), pp. 196–9*)

Certainly, after the freedom of the streets, for the East Ender this was Hell incarnate. Jack London was probably right when he deduced that fear of the workhouse was one of the principal causes of suicide among the working class; while its corollary 'insecurity of food and shelter . . . is a great cause of insanity . . . Costermongers, hawkers, and pedlars, a class of workers that live from hand to mouth more than those of any other class, form the highest percentage of those in the lunatic asylum.' (*London, pp. 268–9*.) Costers (constituting a large part of those classified as 'dealers' by Charles Booth) 'ranked

Orphans in National Children's Home, Bethnal Green, *c.* 1880

Outside the Britannia Theatre, Hoxton Street, *c.* 1907

highest in the street vendors' hierarchy, so when they failed . . . their descent was more agonising. A run of bad luck, a run of bad weather, cholera, disastrous gambling, could unloose a coster's grip on living . . . The final act of despair for a coster was to be forced to apply to the Union . . .' (*Binder, p. 40*)

Even now the wounds inflicted by the workhouse remain embedded in folk memory. Under the comparative benevolence of the Welfare State, there are many old folk, raised in the shadow of the 'Union', who, though in need of extra cash to make ends meet, would rather starve than apply for supplementary benefits. This would make them recipients of government charity (equated, in their thinking, with parish relief) and thereby deprive them of their last vestige of self-respect.

Yet the culture of poverty, gloomy and precarious as it was, was not devoid of relief, expressed in moments of uninhibited joy and the devil with the consequences. What most social investigators failed to perceive was the resilience and humour which sustained most cockneys in adversity. Both Booths identified their fun-making with fecklessness. *Littérateurs* with more catholic perception caught glimpses of the reality. Mackay's monotony of human suffering is briefly transformed by the bright lights of the Whitechapel Road . . . 'the greatest public pleasure-ground of the East End, accessible to all'.

Large musical halls with broad lobbies and high stories and galleries are located there, and small hidden penny gaffs, in which there is little to see on account of the

Night Shelter, Crispin Street

tobacco smoke, and little to hear on account of the noise.—There is the medicine man with his wizard oil which cures all ills,—no matter how taken, internally or externally,—as well as the shooting-stand, whose waving kerosene oil flames make the gaslights unnecessary. There we meet the powerful man and the mermaid, the cabinet of wax figures and the famous dog with the lion's claws—his forefeet have been split; all that is to be seen for a penny.

(Mackay, pp. 171–2)

Margaret Harkness etches in, in greater detail, a host of pleasures afforded by the ever-popular 'gaff' and contributes a rare picture of the more deleterious gin-palace-cum-dance-hall. Local murder and mayhem are always available to provide extra entertainment: 'a murder gives them [East-Enders] two sensations . . .

Was the person poisoned or was his throat cut? Did the corpse turn black or did it keep till the nails were put in the coffin?' Violence, the norm, was ever-present above and beneath the surface, ready to erupt. And when it did, *in extremis*, as in the Ripper murders (1888) and the Sidney Street siege (1911), it created folk legends which persist to this day. Individuals had their hour of glory. Youth's a stuff will not endure, and the young were fully cognisant of its advantages, however ephemeral. For the poor lass 'keeping company' with her man was a public display of a successful catch: the few heady days when, with pride, she could show off her prize, until the prison house of marriage and childbearing closed in. Even then, there could be a temporary escape to the nearby 'cockney' country-side, Wanstead Flats, where on Whit Mondays—

41

... you may howl at large ... the public houses are always with you; shows, shies, swings, merry-go-rounds, fried fish stalls, donkeys are packed closer than on Hampstead Heath; the ladies' tormentors are larger, and their contents smell worse than at any other fair. Also, you may be drunk and disorderly without being locked up—for the stations won't hold everybody—and when all else has palled, you may set fire to the turf.

(*Morrison (2)*)

At the corner of each street was the locus of freedom—the pub—offering nightly its ritual joy session amid the brash glitter and warm camaraderie of the bar; and, within walking distance, was the music hall, where, for a few coppers, one could burst out in a euphoria of collective maudlin or the ribald chorus of a popular song. Always good for a belly laugh, the East End cockney was 'adept at snatching wit from want'. (*Binder, p. 68.*)

Much of this was lost on outsiders—reformers, 'explorers' and saints alike. Even the more astute, like Jack London, Beatrice Webb or Charles and William Booth, heard what they wanted to hear, saw what they wanted to see. The culture of poverty evolves its own, esoteric, responses towards the stranger. For the poorest of East Enders daily engaged in the struggle for life, and razor-sharp in seizing on any advantage, caught on to their 'game' and played along with it for their own profit.

The qualifying images evoked by the social investigators may have been partly illusory. Nevertheless the end product of Charles Booth's pioneer study (*Booth, C. (1)*) by its cold, scientific approach, is convincing. In his quantitative appraisal of Tower Hamlets (population 456,877 in 1887) 35% are categorised as living precariously on or below the poverty line (including 13% defined as chronically distressed 'for whom decent life is not imaginable'), that is almost 160,000 living on the margin. Hunger was the dreaded reality which stalked the streets of East London.

It was, paradoxically, Hitler's *Luftwaffe* that finally put paid to London's Hell's Kitchen. His bombers effected in a few nights what a century of social reformers failed to enact. Much of the slums disappeared beneath the rubble; most under demolition orders from the local authority bent on obliterating the old face of East London. From Aldgate Pump to Bow Bridge, Cable Street to Hackney Road, huge, bright, concrete tenements soar up to cut the skyline. After

Outside 'Itchy Park'

1945 the great Wen had almost, but not quite, been consigned to the dustbin of history. And of that congested human bottleneck of nearly 457,000 souls in 1887, only 146,000 remain.

Certainly hunger and deprivation no longer threaten, except a minuscule group, on whom, some argue, these are self-imposed; no more outcast children and a greater care and respect by the men for their womenfolk. All are well shod (the day of the bootless nipper is over) and the cheap wholesale houses clothe East Ender and West Ender alike, so that, on the streets, the classes are often indistinguishable. The Welfare State has removed for most the once inevitable prospect of want and the fear of old age. The Bastilles are gone, to give way to the offices of Social Security which render a more palatable service when meeting the demands of their 'clients' in need.

Yet the past is as inexorable as the present. Itchy Park (the ever-diminishing gardens adjoining Christ Church, Spitalfields) still persists as a rendezvous for the homeless and destitute, as it was well before its 'discovery' by the Victorian scribes. Mackay's Brick Lane derelict is still around. Even now 'down the side-street a drunken form is feeling its way along a wall, muttering to itself and gesticulating, perhaps over-

Christ Church, Spitalfields, and adjacent gardens (Itchy Park)

Dossers' house, Cleveland Grove

come by a single glass of whisky because the stomach had been without food . . .' (*Mackay p. 170*: a superb description of Brick Lane in 1887. Much of the northern part remains as it was.) Traditionally a magnet for the homeless, this is still aggravated by large numbers of old properties, awaiting demolition and left to decay. With a housing waiting list topping 6,000 (1977), it is reasonable to deduce that the area is not free of overcrowding and that squatters of all kinds will move in to fill up *any* vacant accommodation.

Charles Booth's 'decent life' is now imaginable for the citizens of Tower Hamlets. But attainable for all? Certain quantitative evidence suggests otherwise. Local statistics (supplied by Stephen Carey, Tower Hamlets Borough Council) monitoring areas of 'distress and deprivation' record, for example:

(1) *Children in care on 30 September 1977:*
1,106 – the highest in London.

(2) *Disabled:* 4,073.

(3) *Unemployment at April 1977:*
(a) Poplar Employment Office – 2,325, 14.1% adult males only, i.e. *three* times the national average.
(b) Stepney Employment Office – 2,173, 12.7% adult males only.

(4) *Homeless families – officially aided:*
159 in shorter life property
133 in bed and breakfast accommodation
13 in reception centres
9 in hostel accommodation
13 forced to stay with relatives.
(These are the known 'legal' homeless. What of the unknown who walk the streets seeking a 'doss' for the night in unaided hostel or empty house or tenement?)

Yesterday's mass poverty is gone. Yet, beside the mainstream of a more affluent society, East Londoners still stand apart as a *relatively* deprived and under-privileged community. Pockets of the lost world remain; and a casual stroll through one of the deserted by-ways may suddenly plunge you into the inescapable reality of its past. In garbage-choked Angel Alley by the great library it is no strain on the imagination to conjure up the raucous yells of those mad Irish casuals who, armed with cudgels and knives, for three years held their filthy rabbit warrens against the onslaught of predatory bailiff and police posse; their unpaid rent diverted from the pockets of their landlords to the more insatiable demands of the liquor palace.

In Spellman Street

Foraging in Gunthorpe Street

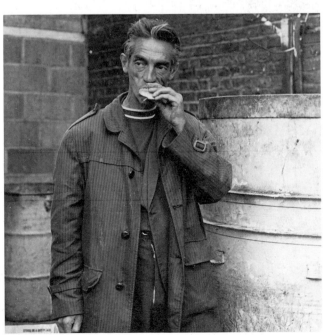

In the Whitechapel Road

47

Gunthorpe Street

Mrs Kandler in Ford Square

PHILANTHROPY

The East End is no stranger to the religious zealot or political ideologue. Nineteenth-century conditions were propitious for attracting both. During the latter part, a company of saints, armed with the Bible and bread basket, marched across the sanitary cordon of Aldgate and plunged eastwards.

It is fashionable to denigrate their 'do-gooding' presumptions, since their passionate moral fervour was tinged with patronising overtones. Yet they chose freely to devote their energies to saving thousands of lives from premature death by hunger and destitution. At the least, in the context of the *physical* salvation of the dispossessed, it is necessary to put the record straight.

Dr Thomas J. Barnardo

One member of the forward echelon of 'saints' was Dr Thomas J. Barnardo (1845–1905).

> In cellar, in garret, in alley and court
>   They weep and they suffer and pine,
> And the wolves of the city are prowling near
>   Back wolves. For the children are mine.

(*Dr Barnardo – Three tracts, 1888*)

Born in Dublin, Thomas John Barnardo was confirmed at 15; but this appears to have had little religious impact on him, since his reading interests were currently limited to secular and revolutionary literature. An innate sense of compassion soon found him teaching in a local Ragged School and visiting sick and poor folk as part-time activities.

In 1865, at a meeting in Dublin addressed by a charismatic speaker, Dr Hudson Taylor of the China Inland Mission, he was so inspired that he resolved to become a medical missionary. He quit Ireland the next year to train at the London Hospital in Whitechapel. Almost immediately he made an impact, not least on the staff. To the wonder, and embarrassment, of his tutors and fellow students, he would set up a platform directly opposite on the Waste, and preach the Christian Witness—to an unappreciative audience. He soon caught on to the terrible social conditions prevailing in that area, especially the appalling incidence of homeless children.

He turned his attention and energy towards succouring them: first physically, then spiritually, on the obvious premise that only the living can be converted. In Ernest Street, Stepney, he founded a Ragged School which he soon transferred to his first children's shelter, a donkey shed in Hope Place, rented at 2s.6d. a week. The floor was laid by a local carpenter, and Barnardo and fellow students set to to renovate the minute premises. They whitewashed and limewashed the walls and rafters, and hung a pair of oil lamps from the roof. Reading texts, Bibles, wooden benches and coal to fuel an old burner were financed out of their own, meagre, income. The shed was open twice a week, including one compulsory attendance for prayers on Sunday.

Local street urchins drifted in, initially drawn by the attractions of warmth, refreshments and shelter rather than, for them, the meaningless Bible readings. Here Barnardo first encountered the bright, homeless boy, Jim Jarvis, who took him on a voyage of exploration through the nebulous alleyways round

Dr Barnardo (1845–1905)

Aldgate. At the end of a narrow cul-de-sac off Houndsditch, Jim directed his attention to the roof of a long shed. Here he found asleep in the cold night air a confused jumble of boys:

> I counted eleven. They lay with their heads upon the higher part and their feet in the gutter . . . some coiled up, some huddled two or three together, others more apart. The rags that most of them wore were mere apologies for clothes. One big fellow appeared to be about eighteen, but the ages of the others varied, I would say, from nine to fourteen.
>
> Just then a cloud passed from the face of the moon, and as the pale light fell upon the upturned faces of those sleeping boys, and I realised the terrible fact that they were absolutely homeless and destitute and were almost certainly samples of many others, it seemed as though God himself had suddenly pulled aside the curtain which concealed from my view the untold miseries of child life upon the streets of London.

His immediate concern was personally to rescue the children, and with the help of Jim he sallied forth nightly on the prowl, gathering up the homeless, and within a few months he had farmed out sixteen lads to foster-parents, their upkeep paid for out of his own pocket. In the long term this was an impossible situation. The first opportunity to publicise and gain funds for his cause came at a conference of missionaries at the Agricultural Hall in Islington. Called to give an impromptu talk on child homelessness, Barnardo broke into an impassioned plea for their aid. The Earl of Shaftesbury, after reading the speech, invited

51

Barnardo to dinner. The same night, at Shaftesbury's demand that he prove his case, Barnardo led the dinner party on a night search for the children's 'lays'. At the *Queens Shades* alley in Billingsgate, they found a group of bodies under tarpaulins, used to cover crates for shipment. A boy was pulled out, and offered 6d. to 'roof' in the 'lay', i.e. to dance on the tarpaulins, thereby waking the sleepers. Seventy-three hungry, frozen, ragged and verminous apparitions came plunging out of cover. Shaftesbury, shocked and moved to tears, declared 'All England should know of this!'

It was a letter from Samuel Smith MP, suggesting that Barnardo cancel his long-term plan to become a missionary to the Chinese and to stay instead in East London and found a home for destitute boys, that gave Barnardo his cue. A donation of £1,000 from the MP would convert this dream into reality.

In 1870, at No. 18 Stepney Causeway, commencing with an initial intake of twenty-five, Barnardo opened his Home for Destitute Boys. The terrible dilemma of choosing five out of the last six vacancies would provide a tragedy which ultimately finalised Barnardo's *raison d'être*. The twenty-sixth boy proved to be John Somers, a red-haired eleven-year-old, nicknamed 'Carrots', who scraped an existence, when he could, as a paper vendor or boot black. He begged to be admitted, but Barnardo reluctantly had to refuse him, not only because the hostel was full, but on the precept that 'Carrots' was the only applicant who, at least, had the (doubtful) privilege of owning a mother. Some days later a Billingsgate porter, on lifting a barrel, dislodged what he thought to be two lads sleeping. One came to life and fled, the other remained motionless. It was 'Carrots': dead of hunger and exposure. The lesson was salutary—for Barnardo. A sign was immediately placed on the front door of No. 18, never to be removed:

NO DESTITUTE CHILD EVER REFUSED ADMISSION

with the addendum beneath:

Open All Night

The iniquities perpetrated against the children of the poor were already legendary when he undertook to expose them consistently until public remedy became imperative. Alone 'the young man with the lantern' prowled the streets at night, through interminable slum courts and alleys, even into the communal kitchens of lodging houses infested by thieves, *procureurs* and prostitutes. He probed everywhere, under barrows, stalls, tarpaulins, into discarded crates and barrels, casting the light of his lantern into the darkest recesses in search of the shelterless child. Soon his intimate acquaintance with the East End nether world revealed the variety of abuses heaped on the young:

Many little female children changed hands in the lodging houses, and experienced untold suffering and wrong in the process. Not only were they often cruelly beaten by their keepers, but not infrequently they were hired or sold as the case might be, to tramps, their parents being the lenders or the vendors. The more pitiful or hopeless the children could be made to appear, the greater was their power to appeal and their ability to excite sympathy and extract the gifts of the benevolent . . .

Instruction in the art of pocket-picking was frequently given by the children's own parents, and many a tiny child looking the picture of innocence was thrust out upon the streets with the stern injunction not to return empty handed . . .

(*Williams*, p. 84)

And finally the most terrible evil 'where inhuman brutes, having secured the custody, for a consideration, of unwanted little ones, took out a policy of insurance on their lives, and then by a subtle process of neglect, ill-treatment and starvation, endeavoured to make sure that no undue length of time elapsed before the sum insured became claimable'.

In one action, by timely intervention, he thwarted the murderous designs on three children by one 'baby-farmer', a ruthless old harridan, who, as each child came into her possession, insured it, pawned its clothes and covered its body in rags.

The Ripper murders (1888) directed public attention towards the social deprivation inherent in East End life. Barnardo, through letters to *The Times* and public speeches, highlighted the moral and physical dangers accruing to children admitted to lodging houses, and advocated the provision of special shelters for young people of the tramp or casual class. Only children under 16 would be admitted, free to enter and depart at will. He revealed that the idea was put to him by a group of terrified women after the discovery of the third murder, during a visit to a lodging house at No. 32 Flower and Dean Street, the notorious criminal-infested thoroughfare off Brick Lane. Four days later he helped identify the remains of the fourth victim, Elizabeth Stride, as one of those women who had strongly advocated his proposals for child protection. He also acted immediately to implement them.

He bought possession of the house in Flower and Dean Street, where Stride had lodged, and a second in Dock Street, and duly licensed them both as Common Lodging Houses for Children. A nominal charge of 1d. per night was made, and a hot meal provided at the cost of a halfpenny. But no child in need was ever denied, even if the penny was not forthcoming. (It was necessary, the Doctor explained, to keep up the form, even to appear inflexible in demanding the night's fee, in accord with current philosophical dictums concerning 'self-help' and unfair competition!) Doors were open nightly at 7.0 p.m. to admit lone children and homeless women with children; a simple, nourishing meal was provided, followed by prayers, and then all retired to bed. At 10.30 p.m. lights were dimmed and the door locked and bolted. But there was no respite from disturbance at night during the current murders. Interminably some lonely and terrified woman would clamour for admission during the early hours; sometimes a policeman would knock and plead shelter for a young girl or child he had found wandering along his beat. None was rejected.

In early days, unscrupulous parents found him an easy touch, but he soon caught on to the situation. They would abuse his trust by agreeing to let him 'rescue' their child and clothe him. A few days later the child would disappear, the new clothes, especially the boots, would be pawned to obtain money for drink. Boots in the East End accorded status (partly confirming one's solvency and, therefore, respectability) and were a saleable commodity. Discovering that many of them ended up in a pawnshop, Barnardo issued them with his stamp for 'hire only' to the parent, so that they always remained his property. If disposed of, the parent could be indicted for theft. It was sufficient deterrent to keep the 'Doctor's children' well shod.

Children's saviour and missionary to the East End heathen apart, Barnardo acted as a practising auxiliary to local teetotalism against the old demon. He set up a Gospel Tent outside the *Edinburgh Castle*, a monumental pub-cum-music-hall in Poplar. The proprietor detected a rapid decline in custom as the hot-gospellers apparently provided more attractive fare and, to cut his losses, he offered to sell Barnardo the business for

£4,000. A public appeal was launched; contributions came pouring in and after a breathtaking race against time—the last £10 being received as the auctioneer's hammer was about to fall—Barnardo became the pub-owner. The Gin Palace and Music Hall was converted into a Coffee Palace and Mission Hall without altering the warmth, colour and bizarre quality of the old establishment. Newspaper and games centres were installed and rooms allocated for Mothers' Meetings, singing classes, Penny Savings Bank, Sick Benefit Clubs, Mission Service and Bible Classes: in all a combination of practical and spiritual beneficence. Among the thousands who came to view the transformed *Castle* was an old black, Josiah Henson, original model for 'Uncle Tom' in Harriet Beecher Stowe's popular classic. In the wider context of social welfare, with this experiment Barnardo emerges as a creator of one of the first community centres.

He also began a school meals scheme. After opening a Free Day School and recognising that it was impossible for children to learn on an empty stomach he introduced free breakfasts and dinners, an innovation which roused the animosity of the current laissez-faire-cum-Samuel-Smiles pundits, who prophesied that moral degeneration would be perpetuated by free hand-outs. By his own admission, Dr Barnardo was never a popular man—with adults. The smug, middle-class Victorians were not amused at his slum-based indulgencies. After all—

> He was their conscience. He brought the smell of the slums into their drawing rooms; he buzzed around them like a mosquito but, unlike a mosquito, he would not go away when swatted. He touched the heart and the pockets of many and fired them with some of his love; he plundered the bank balances of a lot more who only gave in the vain hope that he would stop—stop nagging about his brats, as if *they* were to blame. The man had no taste, no feeling for the fitness of an occasion, and he was Irish to boot.
>
> (*Hitchman, p. 14*)

For the 'brats' were his life, and he poured into them all his mortal care and compassion. After expanding his network of homes across the country to embrace both sexes, he added two naval training schools, a technical school for 300 boys at Golding, Herts., convalescent homes, hospitals and migration training centres. Of necessity he was an authoritarian. He had to organise and direct 102 separate buildings. A creative innovator, he found it difficult to delegate responsibility. Thus he set the pace and strain of superhuman effort which prematurely killed him.

In 1905, when he died, the Homes could tot up 59,384 children recalled to life by his care. That same year 8,000 children were being maintained, of whom 93 of the current intake were crippled, blind or deaf mutes alone. To meet the cost of forty years' intensive labour, £3¼m. was needed and raised by one man. Today the house at 18 Stepney Causeway still stands. It provides more than a legacy and for Barnardo's no 'copyright reserved'. The Stepney model set the pioneer example of orphan care and management whose ramifications have already extended through and beyond national frontiers.

Canon Samuel Augustus Barnett

Toynbee Hall, the Whitechapel Art Gallery and the great Library remain as permanent memorials to the incursion into East London of one of its most 'turbulent priests', Samuel Barnett (1844–1913). It was as missionaries bent on exploration and conversion of the local 'heathen' that both he and his wife Henrietta came to the 'worst parish' in the Bishop of London's diocese. 'We came to Whitechapel attracted by its poverty and ambitious to fight it in its strongest fortress.'

It was, indeed, a tough, almost impossible assignment. The parish chosen, St. Jude's, was probably the most unsalubrious in the metropolis. In 1871 records reveal 'a population of 6,270 (of whom the majority were males) inhabiting 675 houses, many of which were common lodging houses. Through the parish ran a large street, and behind it, both east and west, lay crowded and insanitary courts and alleys . . . The people were dirty and bedraggled, the children neglected, the streets littered and ill-kept, the beer-shops full, the schools shut up.' The vicarage was situated in the heart of the foulest rookeries infested by thieves and prostitutes. A vivid description of their immediate locale is presented by Henrietta Barnett; a nebulous maze which took in the notorious Flower and Dean and Thrawl Street complex (see p. 28 above).

In 1874, an estate agent, an employee of Octavia Hill, pioneer slum demolisher and tenement builder, reports on nearby Angel Alley (part of which still remains) as being in a 'very dilapidated condition, quite

Canon Barnett (1844–1913)

wrecks of houses. It had been sometime a den of wild Irish, but a part of it now is used as stables, and the rest the deputy landlord farms out in what he terms "furnished rooms" . . . He told me of another alley where the people had lived many years without paying rent, for the landlord had deserted them through fear and never being able to get any money. Such was the danger and difficulty of collecting that his wife was then suffering from an Irish attack of poker and broomstick!'

Barnett's initial responses to the appalling degradation seemed hardly motivated by Christian compassion. In accord with the liberal philosophy of the time, self-help was a factor lacking among the poor in their fight for survival. Both Barnetts assessed the poor as partly responsible for their own condition . . . 'We found the poor in want of more adequate relief', but also 'in want of more self-reliance'. To them, spontaneous philanthropy was, in the long term, counter-productive. Early in his ministry (1874) Barnett regarded 'indiscriminate charity among the curses of London . . . I would say the poor starve because of the alms they receive'. The effect is that 'the people never learn to work or to save . . . Out-relief from the House, or the dole of the charitable, has stood in the way of Providence, which God their Father would have taught!' That the poor were primarily victims of market forces operating in a ruthless, laissez-faire milieu does not seem to have occurred to him. Since, among Barnett's somewhat confused moral imperatives, sin was regarded as the most reprehensible of vices, 'the principle of our work is that we aim at decreasing not suffering but sin! . . . In my eyes the pain which belongs to the winter cold is not so terrible as the drunkenness with which the summer heat seems to fill our streets, and the want of clothes does not so loudly call for remedy as the want of interest and culture. It is sin, therefore, in its widest sense against which we are here to fight.' (*Parish report, 1877. Cited in Barnett, vol. 1, p. 75.*) No wonder that the desperate pauper would sooner turn to the warm sympathy of a Salvation Army lassie, or a Charrington who asked no questions in giving, than face the stern pontifications of the priest of St. Jude's.

Yet none of this detracts from his achievements in the long term. For in his time, place and circumstances, Barnett was an innovator in the field of social welfare. He recognised that he was an outsider who could never socially identify himself with the environment, but could only work for its moral and physical regeneration. Arrogant it might be, nevertheless there was a certain honesty in this self-appraisal vis à vis his parishioners. His wife demanded that, in true Christian humility, they share the privations of their flock, and move in among them in Crown Court, a notorious slum alley inhabited by whores and pickpockets. Barnett, after serious consideration, refused: 'For we, conscious of our possessions, would be conscious also that we could step out of the crippling environment at any time. Moreover, we should not have the fear of old age and poverty ever before our eyes.'

Moral improvement would be effected through educational and cultural enlightenment. The old vicarage provided a schoolroom, an adult education centre and a gallery for annual art exhibitions. Barnett was no pedant in the traditional Gradgrind mould which was geared to the accumulation of a dustbin of facts, but a stimulating teacher seeking to draw on the imaginative and creative talents of each individual. Child learning was conducted in a free atmosphere, and craft subjects were compulsory in all curricula, as part aids to vocational training. For the slum child who had never seen a green field, Barnett set up the Children's Country Holiday Fund (1877), a charitable organisation which sponsored annual trips for local youngsters to country villages or the seaside.

It was the successful implementation of three social experiments that projected his name well beyond the frontiers of East London. In 1884 he became the founder warden of Toynbee Hall, an Oxbridge graduate settlement built 'in memoriam' to the work of Balliol historian Arnold Toynbee who had died, prematurely, in 1881. He had preached and practised the gospel of bridging the gap between social classes by urging the leisured educated élite to live and work among the poor, partly as a debt of honour to Labour, the source of all wealth. The warden trained an intake of sixteen graduates and supervised their classes and 'social' duties. He introduced musical concerts, calling on the free aid of West End choirs. Lady Colin Campbell and Madam Clara Butt were among the artistes who sang to packed local audiences at the Hall; lectures by eminent scholars on Milton, Carlyle and Wesley were attended 'by the most 100—or the least 20' (*Barnett*), and R. S. Tawney, Clement Attlee, Alfred Milner and Basil Henriques were, in their youth, dedicated participants in its socio-educational programmes. Toynbee Hall provided the model for a series of university settlements which mushroomed internationally during the last part of the nineteenth century.

Barnett also pioneered the movement for improved housing for the poor. In 1875, the Whitechapel Guardians sent a petition to parliament revealing that the death rate in certain portions of Whitechapel was 40 in 1,000, and that 80% of the paupers came from condemned homes. In that year 'most of the rooms furnished . . . provided a sack of hay, a chair, table and let at 8d. a night' (*Barnett*). They were insanitary, bred disease and were, therefore, a prime cause of the high mortality rate. Barnett saw the problem as threefold:

(a) to get the houses condemned by the local Medical Officer.

(b) thence to induce the authorities to act on this condemnation and demolish.

(c) to find wealthy philanthropists or building companies who would buy the vacant land and erect healthy purpose-built dwellings.

It was this evidence that prompted the urgent passage of the Artisans Dwellings Act of 1875. Yet houses condemned under the Act still persisted in a state of uncertainty for years afterwards. From the explanations posed a century ago, it is curious to note how little has been learned in tackling the same problems today. Thus in the 1870s 'the expectancy of early removal makes landlords unwilling to spend money on necessary repairs and tenants unwilling, by leaving, to miss the chance of compensation'. There is always a time lag between demolition and erection of alternative accommodation—a factor aggravated by the action of the Metropolitan Board who bought up vacant land for speculative deals, rather than for the less lucrative potentials from rehousing the poor.

Whole areas of rabbit warrens came tumbling down; but by 1884 one notes widespread protest over the delay in rebuilding. Vast plots around St. Jude's remained vacant for nine years, except for the erection of two pubs—much to the chagrin of the vicar! In 1883, acting on his own initiative, he brought together in the dining room of the vicarage a group of four public-spirited investors, led by a Mr and Mrs Murray Smith. The result was the formation of the East London Dwellings Company 'to be launched with preliminary promises of £36,000' in order to buy and rehabilitate slum properties. Barnett's concern was to bring shelter to the poorest of the poor on the principle of humane consideration for the individual against the fashionable authoritarian regimentation inherent in the new tenement blocks, structured as lodging 'boxes' for the working class by investors mainly concerned in cheap construction and high profits from rents. He wrote:

> Our intention is to build for the unskilled labourers, the day workers of the docks, and the many men and women who live by casual employment. For such there is as yet no provision by the Building Companies, and the rule of the Peabody Trustees is to admit no tenant who cannot give a reference to a regular employer. We shall have no such rule, we shall let in single rooms, and if possible carry out the plan of having lady rent collectors. If among

these houses of the future there be a common lodging house, without petty rules or unjust interference, it could by its provision for comfort and recreation be an untold advantage to the many who depend for their view of life and course of conduct on the associations of the hotel or common lodging house, in which they are forced to reside.

After a slow start the Four Per Cent Dwellings precipitated its building programme around Spitalfields. By 1886, a jubilant Barnett reports: 'The rebuilding of the poor has been going on apace replacing the net of squalid courts and filthy passages . . . Brunswick Buildings in Goulston Street and Wentworth Buildings in Wentworth Street are inhabited.' The following year, the empty plot which had recently constituted the infamous Crown Court was occupied by the attractive high-rise College Buildings which still stand. Opposite on the north side of Wentworth Street was constructed Lolesworth Dwellings to accommodate 300 families. Barnett's initiative stimulated a spate of local building which included the erection of the Rothschild-sponsored Charlotte de Rothschild group, followed by the Nathaniel block, which replaced the large mass of foul labyrinthine warrens with their troglodyte inhabitants in Thrawl and Flower and Dean Streets.

Barnett used the Ripper murders (1888) to publicise local deprivation and to press for a national effort to rehouse the poor. In a famous letter to *The Times* (19 September 1888) he brought the weight of his experience to bear on the appalling conditions that made crime inevitable in the area, especially Spitalfields: barbed reference was made to the greater criminality prevalent among the West End rich, whose insensitivity and greed were the major contributory causes of poverty and degradation in the East End.

> Whitechapel horrors will not be in vain, if 'at last' the public conscience awakes to consider the life which these horrors reveal. The murders were, it may also be said, bound to come; generation could not follow generation in lawless intercourse, children could not be familiarised with scenes of degradation, community in crime could not be the bond of society, and the end of all be peace . . .
>
> The greater part of Whitechapel is as orderly as any part of London, and the life of most of its inhabitants is more moral than that of many whose vices are hidden by greater wealth. Within the area of a quarter of a mile most of the evil may be found concentrated and it ought not to be impossible to deal with it strongly and adequately. We would submit four practical suggestions.

1. Efficient police supervision. In criminal haunts a licence has been allowed which would not be endured in other quarters. Rows, fights, thefts have been permitted while the police have only been able to keep the main thoroughfares quiet for the passage of respectable people. The Home Office has never authorised the payment of a sufficient force to keep decent order inside the criminal quarters.

2. Adequate lighting and cleaning . . . back streets are gloomy and ill-cleaned. A penny rate here produces but a small sum, and the ratepayers are often poor. Without doubt though, dark passages lend themselves to evil deeds. It would not be unwise, and it certainly would be a humane outlay, if some of the unproductive expenditure of the rich were used to make the streets of the poor as light and clean as the streets of the City.

3. The removal of the slaughter houses. At present animals are daily slaughtered in the midst of Whitechapel, the butchers with their blood stains are familiar among the street passengers, and sights are common which tend to brutalise ignorant natures. For the sake of both health and morals, the slaughtering should be done outside the town. [Butchers Row was near St. Jude's Vicarage.]

4. The control of tenement houses by responsible landlords. At present there is lease under lease, and the acting landlord is probably one who encourages vice to pay his rent. Vice can afford to pay more than honesty, but its profits at last go to landlords. If rich men come forward and buy up this bad property, they might not secure great interest, but they would clear away evil not again to be suffered to accumulate . . .

Henrietta reinforced the plea by organising a petition to the Queen, urging royal aid in improving East End streets ('to close bad houses within whose walls such wickedness is done and men and women ruined in body and soul'), while her husband pressed home the message to landlords that old property was being put to ill use to extort high rents. The difficulty was in tracing the real owners, who, 'when found were, perhaps, respectable parsons or old ladies who had sublet!' The short-term result was that investors shrank from purchasing old property for renovation, but were sufficiently induced to create new companies for demolition and rebuilding. Barnett's efforts bore fruit—particularly among wealthy Anglo-Jewry, whose 4% Industrial Dwelling Company erased vast slum areas and undertook the construction of functional high-rise tenement blocks right across East London.

Most of these are now gone. But from Wentworth Street (Wentworth Buildings) to Stepney Green (Cressy and Dunstan Houses) the legacy remains.

So do others—valuable amenities which have served the local folk to this day. In accord with his aim of educating his flock, Barnett enjoined the wealthy philanthropist, John Passmore Edwards, to finance the first free public library in Whitechapel, which was completed in 1902. Its reference rooms have provided private study facilities, denied them by overcrowded rooms, for Jewish immigrant children, some of whom have gone on to achieve local and national fame. (Among these are included *littérateurs*, poets, artists and mathematicians such as Joseph Leftwich, Isaac Rosenberg, Mark Gertler and Selig Brodetsky.) Crowded in the same rooms now are the new immigrants, Sikhs and Bangla-Deshis, both men and children: the former daily scrutinising their own and English journals, the latter, like their Jewish predecessors, eagerly absorbed in acquiring the host culture. Adjoining the Library stands Barnett's final, and perhaps greatest, contribution to Whitechapel and London—the Whitechapel Art Gallery.

In 1906, Barnett, in recognition of his work, was appointed Canon of Westminster Abbey. He claimed that, in spirit, he never left East London. Certainly his last request was to be buried in the churchyard of St. Jude's. His bodily remains have disappeared in the reconstruction of the East End, which he had striven to bring about. In the company of the saints he stood out as the one 'who had changed the face of East London'. (*Obituary in Daily News, 1913*)

William Booth

It was the Salvation Army, from its inception, that put the East End on the international map; and it was William Booth (1829–1912), with his manifest promise of 'Heaven in East London for everyone', who placed it there.

Booth, the son of a speculative builder, was born at Swinton in Nottingham. His formative years were spent in the security of a middle-class suburb, where, in direct contrast to the nearby city, green fields met the undulating Rudelington Hills, rising in perspective. At 13 he heard the great Chartist, Feargus O'Connor, and became a fervent disciple. Converted to

William Booth (1829–1912)

Wesleyanism at 15, he was similarly infected by the Evangelical zeal of a visiting American Revivalist, the Rev. James Caughey. Both experiences led him towards his future career as a socially-inspired Evangelist; and it was the failure of his father's business in his early youth, and a subsequent *personal* experience of poverty and deprivation, that helped finalise his creed.

In 1848 his first attempts at open-air speaking often ended in disaster. He became the target of a local mob—'the Nottingham Lambs'—who hurled dead cats, stones and bricks at the platform. But his resonant voice and passionate delivery soon prevailed. He even welcomed physical attack which made him more determined to continue, on the precept that since Christ had suffered likewise when preaching His witness, he, too would overcome. Next year, unemployment and the need to feed himself and his widowed mother brought him to London, where for some time he walked the streets, penniless and friendless. Eventually a job as pawnbroker's clerk

(which he loathed) and the heartrending scenes he witnessed there, prompted him to commit all his leisure time to social and mission work among the poor. After a brief spell as a full-time itinerant preacher, and marriage in 1855 to a co-zealous teacher of Evangelism, Catherine Mumford, he advanced (in 1858) to the, then, Methodist New Conversion (Free Church) Group catering to the stern, pietistic demands of its respectable middle-class congregants. Repelled by their complacency and lack of practical concern for the poor, in 1861 he left for London to resume his role as a free-lance Evangelist. He responded to a call from a revivalist sect, operating as the East London Services Committee in Whitechapel. On Sunday 2 July 1865, Booth set up his first platform in a large tent erected on a Quaker burial ground at the Mile End Waste. Thus was launched the Salvation Army. After the usual hostile reception, many who came to mock, stayed to pray, so that Booth could recall:

... before the fortnight had passed I felt at home; and more than this, I found my heart being strongly and strangely drawn out on behalf of the million people living within a mile of the tent ... And so the chapel congregation somehow or other lost their charm in comparison with the vulgar East-Enders, and I was continually haunted with a desire to offer myself to Jesus Christ as an apostle to the heathen of East London.

(*Coates, p. 76*)

In turn, the local heathen was drawn to him by the primitive simplicity of his message, the absence of patronisation and the warmth of informality. He preached joy in giving, in contradistinction to the cold empirical principles applied by the Barnetts to the act of charity, with their dehumanising effect on the recipient. Thus the Salvation Army became 'a cheering presence in the East End, for it never accepted the Victorian idea of the "deserving poor". If a man was poor he was deserving' (*Bermant, p. 104*).

With absolute dedication the pioneers applied themselves without rest under the most adverse conditions. Lacking funds, meetings had to be held in the open air whatever the weather, always nightly, ending at 9.0 p.m. Their first enclosed week night place was 'an old, low warehouse, the windows of which, unfortunately, opened on to the street. When crowded, which was ordinarily the case, it was frightfully hot, especially in summer. If we opened the windows boys threw stones and mud and fireworks

System of beds in early Salvation Army hostel, 1888

through, and fired trains of gunpowder laid from the front door inwards.' Continually forced to change meeting sites, they even conducted services in penny gaffs and covered skittle alleys. Their first breakthrough was the acquisition of the *Eastern Star*—

> a low beerhouse, notorious for immorality . . . We bought the lease and fitted it up. In the front room was our first book store, at the back a good hall, and rooms for smaller classes and meetings upstairs . . . Then came the old Effingham Theatre, on the stage of which there regularly mounted 40, 50 and 60 sinners on a Sunday seeking mercy. In this dirty theatre—at that time perhaps one of the lowest in London—we were fairly introduced to the public, and from that day the work went forth with increased rapidity.
>
> *(Booth, W.)*

Private subscriptions from without and farthing contributions from the poor within the East End, secured Booth the lease of the People's Market in the Whitechapel Road. All-night prayer sessions were inaugurated. 'Experiences' by the saved were openly proclaimed as the mood took them. 'The people spoke as they felt and in the language they knew, and as many of them were totally uneducated the language often sounded strange to cultured ears' (*Coates, p. 89*).

But against the background of hunger and deprivation, street parades, visitations to slums and common lodging houses were subordinated to ensuring that the feeding of the poor was paramount. A programme of cheap food was conceived and kitchens installed where large bowls of soup and chunks of bread were supplied for one penny to the very poor, and for nothing to the penniless. Booth's charismatic presence on the pulpit drew the crowds. Tall, with flowing hair and beard, his piercing eyes beneath the shaggy brows and an impassioned delivery commanded attention and obedience. The movement grew from strength to strength so that, by 1878, it could be suitably re-constituted and titled the *Salvation Army*.

The metaphor was apt. All the paraphernalia of militarism was introduced: uniforms, banners, bands

Salvation Army barracks, from Jack London's *People of the Abyss* (1903)

drilling and marching and the rendering of stirring music, with an authoritarian system of control from the hierarchy downward. Recruitment would be sought among the *lazzaroni*, and he made no compromise with current bourgeois mores when he declared his movement of, and for, the wretched of the earth. He demanded an urgent solution of the social problem as a categorical imperative. 'I claim it for the Lost, for the Outcast, for the Disinherited of the World' (*Booth, W., p. 18*). It was vital that the proletarian army that he had been 'called' to muster, march to Eternal Glory on full stomachs and well-shod feet.

On platform and in print Booth thundered against the social oppressor. The sweater was a prime target, and his criticism sustains itself beyond his time and place:

Those firms which reduce sweating to a fine art, who systematically and deliberately defraud the workman of his pay, who grind the faces of the poor, and who rob the widow and the orphan, and who for a pretence make great professions of public spirit and philanthropy, these men nowadays are sent to Parliament to make laws for the people. The old prophets sent them to hell—but we have changed all that. They send their victims to hell, and are rewarded by all that wealth can do to make their lives comfortable.

(*Booth, W., p. 14*)

He focused attention on the exploitation of women, elevated them within the ranks of his army to man's equal in the fight for redemption:

The lot of a negress in the Equatorial Forest is not, perhaps, a happy one, but is it so much worse than that of many a pretty orphan girl in our Christian capital . . . A young, penniless girl, if she be pretty, is often hunted from pillar to post by her employers, confronted always by the alternatives—*Starve or Sin*. And when once the poor girl has consented to buy the right to earn her living by the sacrifice of her virtue, then she is treated as a slave, and an outcast by the very men who have ruined her!

(*Booth, W., p. 13*)

The lives of Salvation Army lassies ('slum saviours') were often shortened through unlimited devotion to their 'fallen' sisters. Socialist novelist, Margaret Harkness, who spent some years in the East End, observed that 'a slum saviour lives among the filth and the vermin that surround the scum of London. Her work is ignored by the public, who thinks her either a fanatic or a lunatic. Yet she goes about from morning to night nursing the sick, and feeding the hungry with her own scanty rations, until an early death crowns her efforts' (*Law (1), pp. 29–30*). One can accept the evidence of the Angel Alley slum lassie who relates that a dying pauper 'sent for us on her deathbed, *not for Mr Barnett or his curates . . . I daresay Mr Barnett is a good man, but he should go to the West End, where people can understand him*'. A perceptive observation, which could explain why, in times of despair,

the East Ender would turn to the warm ministrations of a Salvationist, rather than the cold comfort afforded by the parson's rhetoric. (There was a slum lassie colony in Angel Alley in the 1880s. The Whitechapel part of the Alley still remains.)

He fulminated ceaselessly against the economic Pharisees, the pundits of 'laissez-faire', calling for public intervention to offset unemployment and other social evils. 'We have had this doctrine of an inhumane cast-iron pseudo-political economy too long entwined amongst us . . . ''Let things alone'', the laws of supply and demand, and all the rest of the excuses by those who stand on firm ground salve their consciences when they leave their brother to sink . . . We want a Social Lifeboat Institution, a Social Lifeboat Brigade, to snatch from the abyss those who, left to themselves, will perish.' Yet, in contradiction, he acquiesced in the

One of the earliest labour exchanges, Whitechapel Road, 1890

Salvation Army, Victoria Home and new Booth House

Social-Darwinism of his time ('I am labouring under no delusions as to the possibility of inaugurating the millenium by any social specific. In the struggle of life the weakest will go to the wall . . . All that we can do is to soften the lot of the unfit . . .'), and emphasised that *he* was not offering a means of transforming society, leaving to 'others the *formulation of ambitious programmes for the reconstruction of our social system*'. In the final count he was less concerned with radical theorising than with the immediate demands of succouring the poor.

In this he was incomparable.

In February 1888, the *East London Observer* reported that a 'former warehouse at 21 West India Docks was opened on the 18th February by General Booth for the purpose of lodging and feeding'. The cost: 3d. a night per bed (plus clean sheets!) with a sleeping capacity for 150 men. There was a good floor restaurant serving a choice of tea or coffee or a basin of soup at $\frac{1}{2}$d. per adult and $\frac{1}{4}$d. per child. Booth's aim was to make it self-supporting. 'Kindred institutions would be established in other poor localities of the metropolis—provision being made for women as well as men.' There were, of course, compulsory prayers and the invitation to be 'saved'. But this new departure in lodging houses served as a model for other public and private constructions (such as the Rowton Houses) while the original 'Sally Army' hostels spread all over the world. For the Commander directed his Army to go forth and redeem sinners everywhere. In 1880 the first missions were set up in the USA, in 1881 in Australia. Through the 1890s settlements spread to India and Ceylon as well as to countries on the European mainland. By 1900 the Salvation Army had come a long way from its primitive beginnings on the Mile End Waste, although, to this day, the principles on which it was conceived remain inviolate. The Salvation Army continues to build. Compare their newest model, 'Booth House', which adjoins the oldest 'Victoria Home for Men'.

Booth's *In Darkest England* is as much a testimony to his success as a testament of belief. Of the nine schemes proposed to alleviate social ills, four have been implemented, i.e. aid centres for prostitutes, ex-cons, drunkards, and above all, the homeless. (Other proposals included the creation of city, farm and overseas colonies to overcome unemployment and the creation of a Whitechapel-by-the-Sea.) He fought ceaselessly for the dignity of Labour. ('A man's labour is not only his capital, but his life. When it passes it returns never more. To utilise it, to prevent its wasteful squandering, to enable the poor man to bank it for use hereafter, this surely is one of the most urgent tasks before civilisation.') Like his fellow voluntarist, Barnardo, he extended the havens of refuge for single mothers and their children. In Clapton he set up a home to receive abandoned babies, or those freely handed over (sometimes in exchange for a few pence) by a starving parent.

Booth must head the list of contemporary 'saints' who gave unstintingly of their labour and devotion to those whom society preferred to ignore. For he and the organisation he created *succeeded* in rescuing from hunger and degradation great armies of the poor, whose numbers extended well beyond the frontiers of London's East End. At the least he fortified its reputation as a haven of caring, where the socially maimed would always find help with compassion, and sympathy with understanding.

Frederick Charrington (1850–1936)

Frederick N. Charrington

The most bizarre benefactor of the East End was its home-born son Frederick Charrington (1850–1936). Heir to the prosperous brewery, based in Mile End, he voluntarily rejected his filial role as inheritor (but not its income!) to pursue the cause of Christ, teetotalism, and the extirpation of vice.

Born in Bow Road, 4 February 1850, educated at Marlborough (where he nearly succumbed to fever) and Brighton College, at 17 he made the 'grand tour' of the Continent, eschewed an Oxbridge education, choosing instead to enter the Mile End Brewery. He was already drawn to evangelism, reinforced by his first experience as a voluntary Bible teacher in a hayloft, where he was surprised to find that he could command the attention and respect of the young toughs. Resolved to soak himself in his environment he took to nocturnal wanderings, where outside Charrington-owned pubs he was shocked into reality by the sight of 'drunken fathers, gin-drinking mothers, ill-used children, whose worst enemies were those whom God designed to be their natural protectors'. He resolved to quit the brewery after viewing a particularly brutal scene enacted outside a Charrington local, the *Rising Sun*:

> As I approached the public house a poor woman, with two or three children dragging at her skirts, went up to the swing doors and calling out to her husband inside she said, 'Oh Tom, do give me some money, the children are crying for bread.' At that the man came through the doorway. He made no reply in words. He looked at her for a moment, and then knocked her down in the gutter. Just then I looked up and saw my own name CHARRINGTON in high gilt letters on the top of the public house, and it suddenly flashed into my mind that that was only one case of dreadful misery and fiendish brutality in one of the several hundred public houses that our firms possessed . . .
>
> What a frightful responsibility for evil rested upon us. And then and there, without any hesitation, I said to myself—in reference to the sodden brute who had knocked his wife into the gutter—'Well you have knocked your poor wife down, and with the same blow you have knocked me out of the brewery business.' (See 'An Oasis in the Desert' report published by *Christian Herald* 1886. The author has often witnessed similar scenes whilst living in the same area during the 1920s and 1930s. W. J. F.)

He moved to rooms at 41 Stepney Green, which he utilised both as living quarters for his personal 'mission' and as shelter for girls in distress. In February 1873, monster crowds converged on the Exeter Hall in the Strand, where the young ex-brewer was elected to preside over the annual meeting of the Band of Hope in aid of temperance. An indifferent orator, his tall handsome Viking-like presence, and not least the legend that he had forsaken £1¼ million for the cause, ensured him a captive audience.

A mission needs a permanent headquarters. A frenetic round of personal and public meetings by Charrington (plus family contributions!) brought in sufficient funds (£8,000) to acquire a site in the Mile End Waste. The foundation stone for a group of buildings was laid by the Earl of Shaftesbury (November 1883), and the final construction formally opened by millionaire colliery owner, John Jory, J.P., on 4 February 1886. The complex, centred on a huge mission hall (The Assembly Hall) which could seat 5,000 people, consisted of a Coffee Palace, a book salon where 'pure' literature was sold, and rooms set aside for the use of Band of Hope, YMCA and YWCA groups. The chairman's opening speech set forth the spiritual and practical aims of the mission's creator:

> 'Mr. Charrington not only offers salvation to the sinner, for he has undertaken operations on a large scale, in periods of distress, to feed the famishing and the starving, and I observe that in a short season of six weeks, six hundred pounds were spent on bread and cocoa. Blessed is he that considereth the poor.'

Henceforth, in accord with the others of the grand local triptych dedicated to saving souls, he succeeded in saving many more bodies from death by hunger.

But the battle for 'purification' was also sustained. This gave legend to the comic-cuts antics Charrington indulged in, in pursuing his own campaign against Sin.

Two hundred yards along the road from the Assembly Hall stood *Lusby's*, a gaudy, brash music-hall-cum-gin-palace, frequented, of course, by prostitutes. (Charlie Chaplin once pounded the boards there. Now an ABC Cinema.) Charrington was resolved to close down, not only *Lusby's*, but all such dens of vice, and so 'rescue', in spite of themselves, the fallen women who frequented them. An extraordinary scene would take place. Bearing a large sandwich board on his shoulders, proclaiming THE WAGES OF SIN IS DEATH and similar homilies, he would march up and down the main road in front of *Lusby's* distributing tracts and exhorting sinners to repent. Suddenly, catching sight of a drunk, swaying in the arms of his 'pick-up'—a local whore—he would confront both with a frenzied outburst, imploring the stupefied 'client' to eschew the Whore of Babylon for the glory of the Saviour. The enraged prostitute would whistle to her bully-boy, standing by in a pre-arranged carriage to take both to her room. The result was a concerted physical assault on Charrington who was often rescued, torn and bleeding, by the timely arrival of a policeman on the beat.

By 1887 the lesson was learned. That year, with reinforcements, and a more subtle approach, he launched his attack on the East End brothels. At night, accompanied by a friend, Charrington prowled through the most dangerous streets, on the hunt for the 'foulest sinks of iniquity'; his weapon—the famous 'black book', in which he entered the name or description of every person (and none was excepted) he saw entering or leaving a brothel. He made it known that the list would be made public and turned over to the police. The result, according to his chronicler, was that

> . . . bullies, the keepers of evil houses, the horrible folk who battened on shame, and enriched themselves with the wages of sin, feared Frederick Charrington as they feared no policeman, no inspector, no other living being . . . The blackest scoundrels in London trembled both at his footsteps and his name.
>
> (*Thorne, pp.159 ff.*)

One victim of the battle for purity was Mrs Rose, 'a procuress and brothel-keeper of the worst description. She was told that Mr Charrington had her name in his "black book" and was coming for the purpose of warning her that he was taking proceedings' (*Thorne, p. 165*). The woman was standing at her door when Charrington approached. Horrified, she fled inside, collapsed in a fit, and died almost immediately. A narrator attributed it to 'the power of God, approaching in the person of His servant . . . that struck down this woman as a terrible example'. Or was it the certainty of retribution under the Criminal Law Amendment Act through its most forceful applicant? Other dramatic incidents, attributed to Divine intervention, occurred. Two girls, rescued by Charrington, were decoyed into a nearby public house, the *Red Cow*, by the publican and imprisoned there all night. Their abductor, known to have publicly cursed and blasphemed against Charrington was found dead next morning. He had poisoned himself.

Inevitably, though unwittingly, Charrington was the instigator of some real life comedies. On one occasion, after summoning some local prostitutes, to show that he was actuated by no animosity he invited them to breakfast with him at the Assembly Hall.

> Twenty-five who had been plying their trade outside the four enclosed houses made their way to the Hall—the majority confessing that their only object was 'to have a lark with Charrington'. Arrived at the small hall, they found two long tables laid out with piles of bread and butter and ham and beef, with two large coffee urns steaming at either end. Mr Day-Winter was sitting at the organ at the time, and by a happy inspiration he proceeded to start the refrain 'For Auld Lang Syne'. The reception was somewhat different from what the women had expected, and after a brief pause of surprise they joined heartily in the refrain. And then they proceeded to attack the viands placed before them . . . It cannot honestly be said that the talk and the general remarks indulged in were of the most carefully chosen or elevating

CHARRINGTON'S MORAL MICROSCOPE

Contemporary cartoon, 1885

character but bad though it was, Mr Charrington and his friends patiently bore it, nor ventured to protest when matters went considerably further, and the coarsest of jokes were cut . . . It was perhaps a mistake—though a well-intentioned one—to start the singing of hymns at the close of the meal: *Sankey's solos and a very recent connection with disorderly houses do not always agree, especially at such short notice!*

> (*Thorne, pp. 163–4*)

Campaigning as Sir Galahad armed with the Gospel, on the quest of saving, often unwilling, 'fallen' women, led him into other hilarious escapades. On one occasion, assisted by two detectives, he burst into a house, in which a young girl was reported to be forcibly detained for immoral purposes. The girl was duly rescued, and on the mantelpiece in the main room of the whorehouse, Charrington was horrified to see his own portrait. The detectives explained that his picture could be found in *every* brothel in East London because 'the keepers of these places wished to have a ready means of identifying the man who was breaking up' their trade.

On Sundays his missionary zeal would reach a crescendo. Headed by Charrington brandishing his inevitable umbrella like a baton, a brass band thumped out popular hymns followed by a procession of the 'saved', carrying banners with boldly inscribed texts and exhorting everyone to join the march. It was a signal for the local drunks to attach themselves, swaying and dancing, to the rear, adding to the cacophony with bawdy music-hall choruses which went ill with the forward party's stern rendering of 'Lead, Kindly Light'; and so the motley parade would wend its way along Sidney Street, across the Commercial Road, through to the Ratcliff Highway en route for Shadwell and Wapping. There was always an encouraging hail from the top window by old Bill Onions, writer of curious doggerel verse, who, now a fervent teetotaller after being imprisoned 480 times for drunkenness, would be summoned every year to the police court of his last conviction to receive the public congratulations of the magistrate!

Seized by an attack of frenzied piety, Charrington would suddenly quit ranks and burst into a dockside pub (his favourite target being *Paddy's Goose*, a notorious rendezvous of 'crimps' and whores), calling on the iniquitous to repent for fear of the Lord, while thrusting in their hands invitations to join his evening service. Such was his fame, and class 'authority', that the outraged landlord dared not protest even when many of his customers, albeit drunk and ready for a bit of disorder, followed Charrington out to add their own raucous enthusiasm to the fun of the march. Thus on return to the Assembly Hall it often required a posse of policemen to prevent an invasion of the Sunday service by the rear end, swollen to a mob of singing drunks!

It is not surprising that there were quite a few eccentrics among the regular preachers invited to address the Sunday meeting. One was 'Hellfire Tom', an erstwhile engine driver on the Brighton line and a fierce drunkard, who had driven his train through the closed gates of a level crossing—a feat which had cost him three months' hard labour. It brought him to Christ and strict teetotalism, and the story of his conversion was a constant repeat item for an apprec-iative audience. Another was the 'returned convict', appropriately named Henry Holloway, who had spent seven years in gaol for burglary, and consequently seen the light. He was specially called on to attract local ex-cons, who guaranteed Charrington a full house, when he was billed to speak.

In spite of many fiascos Charrington appreciated that man cannot live by the spirit alone. Hunger and deprivation were the harsh realities which had to be fought. The 'feeding of the hungry' before any religious service, was, for him, top priority. (*Tower Hamlets Mission*, presently constructed on the same site, continues to adopt the same policy.) Every Sunday, an army of the desperately poor converged on the ornamental gardens in front of the Hall. The first 700 in the queue to attain admission cards were shepherded through the gates by police into the small hall where each received a hot meal, for the price of *signing the pledge*. (Charrington claimed that after personal investigation he found that over 50% permanently kept the pledge.) Closure of the gates was a terrible moment for Charrington. A compassionate man, he was emotionally affected by 'the hopeless despair on the faces of those left in the queue who waited hours for the single chance of a meal, and who must have dispersed unsatisfied'. For his sources of charity were scarcely limitless. By 1912 he was complaining that the current crop of millionaires were not nearly so ready with their cheques as those of the past. 'The great growth of material comfort, the increasing love of magnificence and splendour, seems indeed to have deafened the ears of the very rich to the piteous cry of the starving poor in the East End.'

In the campaign against vice, his success was marginal. By 1888 he had helped to sweep out of existence over 200 brothels and many of the 'rescued' girls were provided for either in his own home for women or at the converted mansion donated by the benevolent Lady Ashburton. He fought a losing battle against the old demon drink. In an attempt to identify and mobilise an international army of abstainers, he minted a badge, specially for the poor, of metal and blue enamel, engraved with the letters BROTA—'blue ring of total abstinence'. A special badge for the rich was manufactured in gold set with diamonds. The latter reflects his fundamental misconception of the underlying causes of poverty and crime, and could explain why his view on ending 'sinful' behaviour by moral persuasion proved invalid. He was tilting at

Inside the Assembly Hall, Mile End Road, *c.* 1890

society's surface manifestations, not its substance. With religion as the panacea, he could neither comprehend nor concern himself with the socio-economic aberrations which perpetuated an uncaring and brutalised society.

But unlike other East End 'saints' the reality of class conflict and a recognition of a developing social consciousness among local labour did not pass him by. He opened the Assembly Hall to the striking match girls (July 1888) as a meeting place, permitting them to gather signatures for the formation of one of the first successful *women's* Trade Unions. On 7 December 1895, the Hall housed a mass meeting (speakers included Eleanor Marx-Aveling and Prince Kropotkin)

called to protest against T.U.C. racist resolutions, passed by the majority, calling for the exclusion of aliens, i.e. mainly Russo-Jewish immigrants fleeing from Czarist persecution. On 8 May 1912, 8,000 Jewish tailors mobilised there to begin their historic strike against the sweating system; and in that same hall, during the second great Dock Strike of 1912, Charrington organised and supervised the feeding of hungry strikers' families. When the time came, he was actively on the side of the dispossessed.

The irony is, that while *he* was soon forgotten, Charrington's brewery, which he had rejected and fought so hard to destroy, has grown from strength to strength. Yet his memory can never be erased from the annals of simple men who elected to devote their lives to the service of the poor. In the final count his record will stand the test of his convictions. In the East End he fed the hungry, fought an endless battle for the liberation of its women from exploitation and prostitution, gave practical aid to workers engaged in the struggle for social rights, and, in a milieu of harsh utilitarianism, preferred charity with a human face.

It could be argued that while the Christian ethic motivated Booth, Charrington and the like, they were engaged in treating only the symptom, not the disease. All rejected political action; nor could they contemplate a radical transformation of society in secular terms. Yet there were priests who did. Charles Kingsley and his group had juxtaposed Socialist and Christian principles in formulating their own criticism of society. They were a thorn in the side of the Establishment. For socialist commitment inevitably found them on the same platform as atheists and other anti-clericals. For them the 'Empire of Hunger' offered a practical opportunity for personal involvement in social crusades.

The Rev. Stewart Headlam (1847–1924) was one of this breed. While serving his apprenticeship as a curate in Bethnal Green in 1887, he founded an active radical Anglo-Catholic group—the Guild of St. Matthew. That same year he roused the anger of his bishop by a speech calling for a more sympathetic appreciation by the clergy of theatre and music halls, and he was duly sacked. Undeterred, he went on to establish a Church and a Stage Guild, to act as liaison group and to encourage a permanent dialogue between the two. A private income enabled him to offer full-time service to any cause he espoused.

This maverick priest manifested extraordinary courage by his idiosyncratic behaviour during certain scandals. In 1880 he sent a telegram of support 'in the Name of Jesus Christ the Emancipator' to the notorious anti-religious Charles Bradlaugh for his refusal to take the Christian oath, incumbent on all MPs; and in 1895 he offered bail for Oscar Wilde, currently on trial for homosexual offences and the object of universal execration.

But it was his successful incursion into East End radical politics that confirmed him in his role as anti-Establishment priest fighting the more practical, secular battles for his flock. He openly took his stand for the deprived against the privileged. He allied himself to any movement or organisation which advocated his views, in turn supporting the Fabians and the SDF while contributing articles to *Justice* and the *Church Reformer* on the way. His efforts were directed towards educational reform, which he believed *could* help redress the balance of opportunity in favour of the poor; although, with political insight, he was less optimistic about its ability to effect social change. As long as control was invested in the hands of a ruling minority, a revised school system would never transform society. But it could intensify the demands of the under-privileged as they were made more aware of the injustices perpetrated against them.

The message was underlined in his address as radical candidate in the famous London School Board election of 1888. He called for free schools and free dinners, to be financed out of taxation imposed on the wealthy landlord and industrialist. Schools needed to make children critically aware of society's shortcomings:

> . . . above all to make them discontented with the evil circumstances which surround them. There are those who say that we are educating your children above their station. That is true; and if you return me I shall do my utmost to get them such knowledge and such discipline as will make them thoroughly discontented, not indeed with that state of life into which it shall please God to call them, but with that evil state into which anarchy and monopoly has forced them, so that by their own organised and disciplined effort they may live fuller lives than you have been able to live, in a more beautiful world than you have had to toil in. (See his election address in *Justice*, 17 November 1888, and the *Church Reformer*, December 1888)

A call for political indoctrination or a plea for a social 'awareness' programme? Stewart Headlam threw out the challenge—and the debate continues.

What appealed to Hackney electors was his proposal that, as a major employer, the School Board should guarantee union rates of pay for their workers. The result was overwhelming Trade Union support, and his election as one of the first two radicals to sit on the London School Board. There he continued as member until 1904, and after 1907 he served on the London County Council until his death in 1924. But his primary concern remained with educating the poor. The East End acknowledged their debt by perpetuating his memory through the Stewart Headlam Primary School erected in Whitechapel.

More pertinent was the recognition that he appealed to the unity of Christian and egalitarian principles and embodied them in his crusade of social action. He was the progenitor of a line of radical priests, who hand on the crusader's sword, one to another, each driving harder, if not faster, towards that seemingly elusive goal—the social transformation of East London. The continuity is evident. A galaxy of turbulent clerics whose most recent exemplar, Trevor Huddleston, is probably the brightest star of them all.

In the inter-war years the connecting link was the equally charismatic son of the Community of the Resurrection, Father St. John Groser (1890–1966), of whom right-wing prelates and laymen, in a Chestertonian adaptation, would lament:

> God made the wicked Grocer
> For a mystery and a sign . . .

For forty years (1922–62) the tall, white-haired, flowing-cassocked priest strode purposefully through East London streets, emphasising the indivisibility of Christ's witness and the Socialist Kingdom, but always translating the message, where possible, into direct action. In 1926, he walked forward, alone, to try to deter a police unit massing to attack a crowd peacefully assembled outside the Poplar Town Hall to hear the proclamation of the end of the Strike. He was felled to the ground by a baton, his arm broken. The Church Establishment was neither sympathetic nor amused, and for nearly two years (1927–8) he was virtually unemployed, supporting himself by occasional paid duties and mainly engaged in sharing his concern and meagre income with the sick and needy of the parish. Relief came with the offer of a temporary living at Christ Church, Watney Street, a mouldering edifice and a nearly defunct congregation. With a team of volunteers the new curate-in-charge embarked on an experiment in self-help: the interior was renovated and remodelled, to which his own skill as a weaver contributed vestments and frontals of liturgical colours. The socialist priest had found the natural habitat for exercising his own interpretation of Evangelism.

A spectacular build-up of worshippers within the year brought the offer of a permanency. The radical image of the minister was soon projected beyond the East End. Friends, left-wing secularists and Catholic Crusaders, would flock to his Sunday services and there sturdily render together

> God is the only landlord
> To whom our rents are due.
> He made the earth for all men
> And not for just a few.

to the tune of 'We plough the fields and scatter'!

For him prayer and action were integral parts of the fight for social justice and for thirteen years he participated in every facet of socio-political activity in the East End. Not only could he be seen on street-corner platforms (he was a splendid orator) hurling his polemics, always tinged with Biblical allusions, against the evils of the Means Test or Mosleyite racism, but he was also practically employed as Chairman of the local Public Assistance Committee in humanising poor relief or, in his finest hour, as President of the Stepney Tenants Defence League in the Rent strike movement (1938–9) which led to a wholesale reduction in rents and the improvement in physical conditions of slum tenements. The legendary picture remains in folk memory: of the militant priest at the barricades erected to resist the onslaught of police and bailiff, carried shoulder-high by the tenants at the hour of victory.

Such was the legacy left to his spiritual successor in the changing milieu of post-war Stepney. St. John Groser up-dated the role of radical Christianity, and adopted it as a gage of battle for the social amelioration of his flock. In 1966 he died.

In 1968 Trevor Huddleston moved into the house at 400 Commercial Road as Bishop of Stepney. The battle was recommenced.

The latest 'turbulent priest' started with the advantage of international fame (his personal, courageous involvement in the fight against apartheid in South Africa is movingly recorded in his *Naught for*

Trevor Huddleston

your Comfort) and, in a sense, he still views problems peculiar to the East End (especially those resulting from immigration) in a global context. However, most of his energies have been bound up in consolidating and extending changes attained by his predecessors, as well as in a pragmatic day-to-day watch on the interests of each *individual* in his diocese. In this he can call on powerful aid which he employs constantly—the media. It is an exercise in mutual aid. Radio and television exploit his talents as a charismatic and controversial figure who can always command an audience, while he makes full use of them for his own ends.

On the streets, the tall, ascetic figure is instantly recognisable at the forefront of demonstrations called to protest against anti-immigration, unemployment or appalling housing conditions. From a secular view he is motivated by a passionate concern for the dispossessed, and a concomitant loathing for injustice perpetrated against those least capable of resisting.

Lining up at Victoria Home,
the first Salvation Army hostel

Reception, Victoria Home
Kitchen, Victoria Home

He regards Socialism as the practical working out of Christian philosophy in this world; his dictum is in accord with that of the 1967 Arusha Declaration of his friend Julius Nyrere:

> The basis of Socialism is a belief in the oneness of man and the common historical destiny of mankind. Its basis, in other words, is human equality. The justification of Socialism is Man . . . Socialism is not for the benefit of black men nor brown men nor white men nor yellow men. The purpose of Socialism is the service of man, regardless of colour, size, shape, skill, ability or anything else.

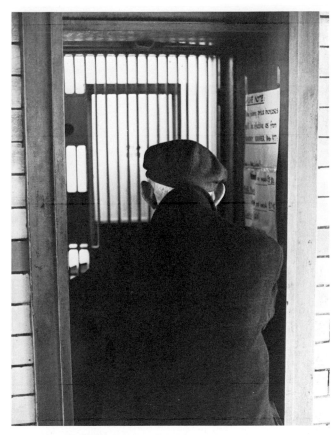

With this universal definition he combines the activities of his 'saintly' precursors. With Barnardo he shares a practising concern for deprived children. His house in Commercial Road is often filled with youngsters. ('Children knock at the door and say they just want to see the Bishop!'); on some week-ends, he might be seen in full regalia, poised behind the wheel to transport a carful of laughing nippers to the coast— for some their first sight of the sea.

Like Barnett, he views present housing deficiency as

In the courtyard, Victoria Home

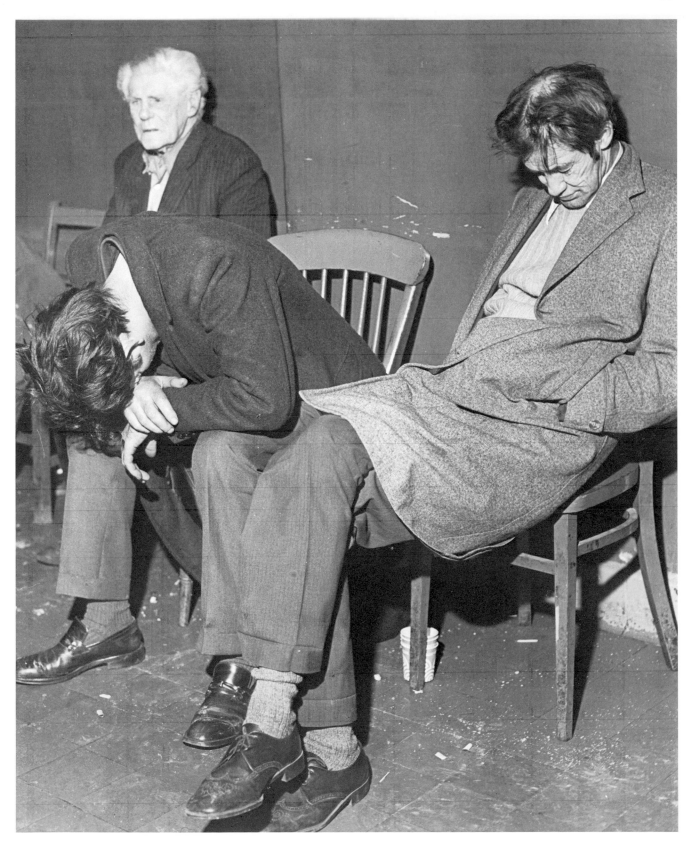

In the basement, Victoria Home

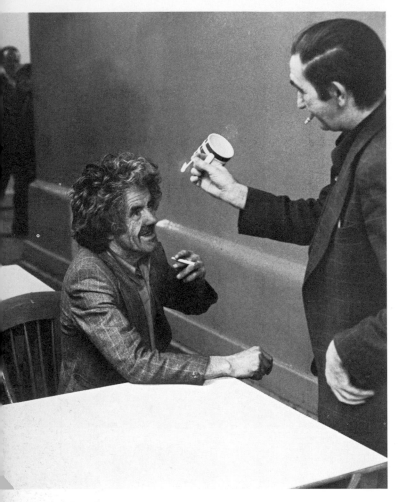

In the dining room, Victoria Home

Reception, Booth House

a major scar on the face of East London, but sees that substituting high-rise tenements to effect mass accommodation or 'transportations' to the new towns, were tragic errors. For in old Stepney the collective spirit was born out of a street culture based on the pub, the all-purpose corner store, the neighbour with the ever-open door, and sustained by root feelings of continuity and community. The massive boxes brought a sense of powerlessness, of alienation. Greater development exists, and with a programme geared to renovation and renewal of viable old low-storeyed dwellings and a more sensitive creativity applied to new building, the East End would reclaim its historic identity.

For Huddleston, all forces must be harnessed to protect the individual, whether it be in house conservation (especially where an old tenant appears defenceless against his landlord) or in rendering immediate help to a family where its breadwinner has

been consigned to prison. He appeals for positive reforms, and, where possible, implements them within the bounds of his own jurisdiction. He has already fulfilled one of St. John Groser's suggestions, first mooted in 1930, of recruiting and ordaining worker priests from the ranks of East Enders. In drawing on his experience of Africa, he has gauged the feasibility of nourishing the leadership from the grass roots. He has always claimed that there is a reservoir of talent among local folk, which the Church will ignore at its peril.

After ten years he has left for his new ministry: Mauritius, with a potentially multi-racial society for which he has fought. Whether his successor joins the 'saints' or not, the East End will no doubt find its own way of sustaining the tradition whilst the old image manifestly persists.

Canteen, Booth House

IMMIGRANTS

After the sixteenth century, Tower Hamlets, strictly limited westward by the bounds of the City, but rapidly developing eastwards with the expansion of the Port of London, provided an *entrepôt* for successive waves of foreign immigrants. The Huguenots in the seventeenth century were followed by the Irish in the eighteenth and nineteenth centuries; and between 1870 and 1914 East London experienced the greatest influx of 'strangers' until the Commonwealth influx after 1945.

During the eastern European immigration over 120,000 mainly Russian and Polish Jews constituting the most dispossessed and impoverished of the European proletariat, according to Karl Kautsky (1901), came to seek asylum here, fleeing from the worst persecution of their people until the Nazi holocaust. (The 1901 Census registers 95,425 'Russians and Poles'—which means the Russian and Polish *Jews* settled in Britain. In 1911 the numbers stood at 106,082. On top of this must be added approximately 20,000 German, Austrian, Dutch and Rumanian Jews who entered Britain after the turn of the century.) A nucleus of Jews was already domiciled in the Aldgate and Minories area by the eighteenth century. By 1850 the ghetto was firmly established around the focal point of Petticoat Lane with some offshoots extending into the narrow alley-ways beyond the confluence of the Whitechapel and Commercial Roads. After 1881 the 'alien invasion' rapidly increased as a result of government-sponsored pogroms against the Jews in Western Russia. Henceforth the ghetto expanded across Spitalfields so that by 1889 Charles Booth could report:

The newcomers have gradually replaced the English population in whole districts which were formerly outside the Jewish quarter. Formerly in Whitechapel, Commercial Street roughly divided the Jewish haunts of Petticoat Lane and Goulston Street from the rougher English quarter lying in the East. Now the Jews have flowed across the line; Hanbury Street, Fashion Street, Pelham Street, Booth Street, Old Montague Street, and many streets and lanes and alleys have fallen before them; they fill whole blocks of model dwellings; they have introduced new trades as well as new habits and they live and crowd together *and work and meet their fate independent of the great stream of London life surging around them.*

(*Booth (2), vol. I, see Webb, ch. 2*)

As the Jews pressed eastward so did their life style begin to project a bizarre quality onto the immediate environment. Slowly the narrow streets and court-yards of Whitechapel, Mile End and St. George's filled up with *Landsleit* (families emanating from the same town or village in Russo-Poland). They formed their own self-contained street communities with work-shops, *steibels* (small, house-based synagogues), and all-purpose stores where the men would foregather on Sundays to discuss the rabbi's sermon, politics and local scandal, or indulge surreptitiously in the immigrant's vice—gambling. During the whole life of the East End ghetto the familiar figure of the 'bookie' (bookmaker), recognised at close quarters by his loud, outlandish clothes and rubicund bonhommie, could be seen working his pitch outside some corner shop. On Fridays, the eve of Sabbath, the cloistered alleys and thoroughfares came to life as candles blazed from the front parlours of shabby one-storeyed

Surviving Huguenot shopfront, Artillery Lane

Jewish immigrant couple, *c.* 1900

Old Sikh in Princelet Street

cottages or tenements. In their weekend finery, the reluctant youth of both sexes were led to *shool* (synagogue). On high holy days the young men, garbed in dress coats and flaunting their manhood along the main streets and high roads of the ghetto, 'were epitomes of one aspect of Jewish history, replacing the primitive manners and foreign piety of the foreign Jew by a veneer of cheap culture and a laxity of ceremonial observance'. During the week they laboured at the bench or behind the machine of the sweatshop. The weekend spelt freedom when the young escaped from parental restraints to the gay vulgarity of the *Pavilion* or *Shoreditch* music hall, or, more daringly, to the local dance hall catering for a mixed clientele. Here sex play was more open, and cross-ethnic relationships loosely established. Yet with all these illicit temptations, the young man stayed tethered to his people, since 'whether he married in his old station or higher up the scale, he was always

faithful to the sectarian tradition of the race, and this less from religious motives than from hereditary instinct' (*Zangwill, p. 237*). While the first-born generation viewed themselves as Britishers with pride, the old, like the immigrant Reb Shmuel, could 'never quite comprehend the importance of becoming English. He had a latent feeling that Judaism had flourished before England was invented' (*Zangwill, p. 103*).

For those who had just arrived or were impervious to change and circumstance, the *stiebel* sustained their ambiguous response to the new environment. It was a confirmation of their identity in *goles* (exile) yet reflected a poignant attachment to the *heim* which had dealt with them so harshly. (*Heim*—homeland, i.e. Russia or Poland. The early immigrants still thought of returning to a free homeland.) By 1889 Beatrice Webb confirmed that these *chevras* (religious associations) supplied 'the needs of some 12,000 to 15,000 foreign

Jews . . . [they] combine the functions of a benefit club for death, sickness and mourning rites with that of public worship and the study of the Talmud. Thirty or forty of these *chevras* are scattered throughout the Jewish quarters . . . Usually each *chevra* is named after the town or district (e.g. the Poltava Synagogue late of Heneage Street off Brick Lane) in Russia or Poland from which the majority of its members have emigrated . . . from ties of relationship or friendship or, at least, from the memory of a common home—that the new association springs'. Even she responded in some degree to the emotional manifestations of the participants. 'Here, early in the morning or late at night, the devout members meet to recite the morning and evening prayers or to decipher the sacred books of the Talmud. And it is a curious and touching sight to enter one of the poorer and more wretched of these places on a Sabbath morning.' But it is Israel Zangwill, who was involved and understood, who presents the reality with an amalgam of wit and pathos unrivalled in its imagery:

> The *stiebel* (consisted of) two large rooms knocked into one, and the rear partitioned off for the use of bewigged, heavy jawed women who might not sit with the men lest they should fascinate their thoughts away from things spiritual. Its furniture was bare benches, a raised platform with a reading desk in the centre, and a wooden curtained ark at the end containing two parchment scrolls of the Law, each with a silver pointer and silver bells and pomegranates. The scrolls were in manuscript, for the printing press had never yet sullied the sanctity of the synagogue editions of the Pentateuch. The room was badly ventilated, and what little air there was was generally sucked up by a greedy company of wax candles, big and little stuck in brass holders.

Here the worshippers came:

> . . . two and often three times a day to batter the gates of heaven and to listen to sermons more exegetical than ethical. They dropped in, mostly in their workaday garments and grime, and rumbled and roared and chorused prayers with a zeal that shook the window-panes, and there was never lack of a *minyan*—the congregational quorum of ten.
>
> This synagogue (Sons of the Covenant) was all of luxury many of its Sons could boast. It was their salon and their lecture hall. It supplied them not only with their religion, but their art and letters, their politics and their public amusements. It was *their* home as well as the Almighty's, and on occasion they were familiar, and even

'Shewshiks', famous Jewish ritual and steam baths, Brick Lane, *c.* 1900

> a little vulgar with Him. It was a place in which they could sit in their slippers—metaphorically, that is; for though they frequently did so literally, it was by way of reverence, not ease. They enjoyed themselves in this *Shool* of theirs; they shouted and skipped and shook and sang, they wailed and moaned; they clenched their fists and thumped their breasts, and were not least happy when they were crying. There is an apocryphal anecdote of one of them being in the act of taking a pinch of snuff, when the confession caught him unexpectedly.
>
> 'We have trespassed', he wailed mechanically, as he spasmodically put the snuff in his bosom, and beat his nose with his clenched fist.
>
> (*Zangwill*, pp. 254–6)

The 'new' immigrants of today—the West Indians in their home-spun Revivalist chapels—would know what this is all about. For the rejected and dispossessed the language may be different, but the liturgy is the same.

Immigrant *Seder*, c. 1900

The *stieblech* persisted as the synagogues of the immigrant poor. Their own *heimische* (i.e. from their homeland—Russia or Poland) rebbes married and buried them. Establishment Anglo-Jewry's *United Synagogue* was anathema to them—its proud, elegant Chief Rabbi indistinguishable from the *goyishe* Archbishop of Canterbury. His aloof, patronising demeanour, his consistent opposition to Yiddish language and culture and, above all, his acolytes' anglicised 'deviation' from age-old ritual, helped sustain this animosity. It led to the foundation of the separatist *Federation of Minor Synagogues* (1887). In 1898 the immigrant ultra-orthodox *Machzikei Hadath* (Upholders of the Religion) had sufficient funds to acquire the great Huguenot church in Fournier Street, and transformed it into the principal synagogue of the East End, where the 'truly' orthodox could worship and study. With the Jews replaced by the new immigrants—Indians and Bangla Deshis—since 1977,

this has been bought by the latter and transformed into a mosque.

Economically the life of the 'greener' (newcomer) was one of grinding poverty, of unremitting labour in the sweatshops which had sprung up, from Spitalfields eastwards, in the small streets adjoining the two main thoroughfares and southwards towards the docks. Within the job market, the immigrant found himself faced with a number of harsh realities. Physical conditions of labour were, to say the least, socially and medically hazardous. Workmen slept in the workrooms, particularly the new arrivals with no fixed abode, and breathed in an atmosphere already foetid with the sweat of congested day-workers and the steam of the press irons. Opportunities were strictly limited. The system was periodically choked with high static and frictional unemployment. Every year, the inevitable gap between 'busy' and 'slack' season brought the threat of homelessness and hunger. For the ordinary Jewish workman this spelt out a precarious living, always poised on the margin of subsistence. The difficulties of adjustment to this new land, the tensions inherent in insecure employment, the financial and legal problems to overcome before he could bring over his family from the *heim* forced him into an unlimited application to work.

The new dimension of freedom provided additional momentum for the fulfilment of one's innate potentiality, which, in the immigrant's rationale, would be directed towards material success as a pre-requisite for security. For most it proved elusive. The ease with which workman became master and vice-versa is legendary. The would-be entrepreneur turned his living room into a workshop, with a friendly landlord or storekeeper pledged as security. He would call on the aid of a brother Jew (whose task was to supply pattern garments to wholesalers) for a price. With a

Outside the Pavilion theatre, *c.* 1900

A tailor's workshop before 1914

The Cheepers, Jewish immigrant family, 1911

small down-payment he obtained hire of a sewing machine and pressing and tailor's tables. Booth records:

> At first, the new master will live on green labour; will, with the help of his wife or some other relative, do all the skilled work that is needed. Presently, if the quantity of his work increases, or if the quality improves, he will engage a machinist, then a presser. His earnings are scanty, probably less than those of his skilled hands to whom he pays wages, and he works all hours of the day and night. But the chances of the trade are open to him; with indefatigable energy and with a certain measure of organising power he may press forward into the ranks of the large employers, and if he be successful, day by day, year by year, his profit increases and his labour decreases relatively to the wages and the labour of his hands.
>
> (*Booth, C. (2), p. 232*)

But only a ruthless minority made it. Until the 1930s the tragicomedy would be repeated *ad nauseam*. The majority who tried suffered their dubious hour of glory as master and then sank back into poverty and debt. In the jungle of cut-throat competition which proliferated, they were overwhelmed one by one.

After an initial sympathetic reaction towards them as victims of pogroms, etc., the immigrants soon found they had few friends. Anglo-Jewry regarded them as an imposition, at a point where the native-born had made a final breakthrough in their efforts to integrate, though they were forced into an ambivalent response—that is, to offer positive aid traditionally accorded to co-religionists. On the one hand they funded advertisements in Yiddish for the Russian press to warn off Jews from emigrating to Britain, or on arrival exhorted them to return or, with part aid, hustled them on to the States or Canada. However, for those forced to stay, Anglo-Jewry provided two centres offering ad hoc hospitality to the poor and weary 'greener'. Such were the Poor Jews' Temporary Shelter (established October 1885, in Leman Street near to the docks, and subsequently still operating in North London) and the Jewish Board of Guardians. The former developed as an entrepôt, welcoming the newcomer and operating as a dispersal agency in which the immigrant was protected from dockside *crimps* or land sharks. From its inception it worked in close co-operation with local and government authorities and thus attained official respectability.

During the 1880s, anti-alien sentiments with strong anti-semitic undercurrents gathered pace. For those Londoners who faced the expanding ghetto with its peculiar sub-culture, the growing fear and dislike for the bizarre invaders would be appropriately utilised: by demagogues seizing on the traditional scapegoat, politicians on the make, or trade union leaders (albeit ill-informed and prejudiced) who viewed their coming as a threat to the livelihood of their members. In *The Dock Labourer's Bitter Cry* (1889) Ben Tillet voiced the Irish-cockney reaction to the Jew in language reminiscent of that which had been used against his own father—an Irish immigrant forced to emigrate to Britain to seek bread and work:

> . . . the influx of continental pauperism aggravates and multiplies the number of ills which press so heavily upon us . . . Foreigners come to London in large numbers, herd together in habitations unfit for beasts, the sweating system allowing the more grasping and shrewd a life of comparative ease in superintending the work.

The *Pall Mall Gazette* (February 1886) had first focused the issue with a virulent attack on the alien 'menace' in the East End. It openly referred to 'A *Judenhetz* brewing in East London', deduced from a letter it had received warning its readers that 'the foreign Jews of no nationality whatever are becoming a

Jewish soup kitchen, Brune Street

pest and a menace to the poor native born East Ender' in that 'fifteen or twenty thousand Jewish refugees of the lowest type . . . have a greater responsibility for the distress which prevails (there) than probably all other causes put together'! The ball soon entered the political arena. Following a year of the greatest economic depression, on 10 March 1887, Captain Colomb, Conservative MP for Bow and Bromley, put the question to the House of Commons and set the tone for future generations of exclusionists:

What great states of the world other than Great Britain permit the immigration of destitute aliens without restriction; and whether Her Majesty's Government is prevented by any Treaty obligations from making such regulations as shall put a stop to the free importation of destitute aliens into the United Kingdom.

With unemployment as a major pressure gauge, 1887 was the year of opportunity both for political demagogues flying the anti-alien kite and for the new social reformer. The old scapegoat was available and

Defunct Jewish corner store, corner of Gun Street and Artillery Lane

the government responded to the populist mood from below. In February 1888 it appointed a House of Commons Select Committee to report on Immigration, paralled by a House of Lords Committee to investigate Sweating (popularly identified as an immigrant importation). The outcome of the Commons' report proved inconclusive. The Committee expressed no urgent need for legislation but resurrected some antiquated clauses from an act of William IV to quantify all future immigration.

By 1888 prejudice had broken surface. Political agitators were already mouthing rhetoric derived from the lowest common denominator—the irrational fears and hatred festering in the mind of the slum-dweller. The Whitechapel murders of that year provided the setting for a minor outbreak of Judophobia. After the third Ripper murder a local editor observed under the heading 'A riot against the Jews':

> On Saturday in several quarters of East London the crowds who assembled in the streets began to assume a very threatening attitude towards the Hebrew population of the District. It was repeatedly asserted that no Englishman could have perpetrated such a horrible crime as that of Hanbury Street, and that it must have been

done by a *Jew*—and forthwith the crowds began to threaten and abuse such of the unfortunate Hebrews as they found in the streets. Happily the presence of a large number of police ... prevented a riot actually taking place.

(*East London Observer*, 15 September 1888)

The aftermath of mass expulsions from Moscow and Kiev with a rising rate of unemployment in the 1890s dramatised the issue again through a vociferous outburst of anti-immigrant propaganda. Agitation against the 'destitute alien' grew in volume and intensity, 1892 being a peak year which registered the first large-scale entry of the problem into active politics.

The impetus towards restrictionism brought to-gether strange bedfellows: Conservatives and Imperialists on the one hand, Radicals and Trade Unionists on the other. A popular cry for the vote catcher had arrived. Immigrants were accused of depriving host workers of jobs, houses; of overcrowding in insanitary conditions; of introducing nihilistic ideas and pursuing a religion which was inconsistent with the British way of life. One Christian gentleman suggested that only the effect of a forced exodus could bring relief to his East End parishioners 'when thousands of the race that spoiled the Egyptians journeyed down the broad streets to the docks of Poplar' (*Reaney, pp. 87–92*). Gentile Trade Union leaders were galled by their ineffectual attempts to combine in order to resist sweatshop conditions, labouring the fact that a constant inflow of foreigners who had never experien-

The Miah family

ced Trade Union activity could only postpone conditions for a stable combination in trades. After sporadic attempts at the formation of a national movement, in 1900 a British Brothers League was founded in East London, whose ideology foreshadowed that of the Mosleyite Fascists. As a result of prejudice, vicious accusation and the pressure of opportunist MPs led by the Tory MP for Stepney, Major Evans Gordon, the drive towards exclusion gathered momentum. On 29 January 1902, Evans Gordon moved an amendment to the Queen's Speech in which he painted a lurid picture of Stepney resulting from the 'alien invasion' and warned of the consequences of uncurbed immigration:

In *Bloom's*

These are the haunts of foreign prostitutes and *souteneurs* of gambling dens and disorderly houses . . . The working classes know that new buildings are erected not for them but for strangers from abroad; they see notices that no English need apply placarded on vacant rooms; they see the schools crowded with foreign children and the very posters and advertisements on the walls in a foreign tongue; they see themselves deprived of their Sunday for that too is gone, and it is no longer within the power of an English working man in many parts of East London to enjoy his day of rest . . . *A storm is brewing which, if it be allowed to burst, will have deplorable results.*

An extravaganza strangely similar to that thought up by the ex-MP for South West Wolverhampton sixty-six years later! (Enoch Powell's speech in Birmingham, 20 April 1968. He took his stand as a

Sid Bloom

defender of the native English people and culture who 'found themselves made strangers in their own country. They found their wives unable to find hospital beds in childbirth, their children unable to obtain school places, their homes and neighbourhoods changed beyond recognition, their plans and prospects for the future defeated.' He added: 'It is like watching a nation busily engaged in heaping up its own funeral pyre . . . As I look ahead, I am filled with foreboding. Like the Romans, I seem to see the Tiber foaming with much blood!') Evans Gordon was quite wrong, in one respect totally so. For the newcomers aroused the special hatred of that class of ladies of the night, who, as the Jews moved in quickly, experienced a dramatic drop in custom. In the long term tough Jewish puritanism proved formidable against its more permissive antagonists. The *demi-monde* could see no pleasure or profit in remaining and took off to more lucrative areas; so much so that by 1907 the Rector of Spitalfields could report with satisfaction that much of his domain had been cleared of vice, thanks to his non-Christian parishioners! Anti-alienism prevailed. The first Aliens Bill aimed at restricting entry was debated furiously, passed and made law on 1 January 1906. Up to 1914 the influx of immigrants was reduced to 4,000 a year. When war broke out immigration had virtually ceased and the East End ghetto had consolidated itself with numbers amounting to over 100,000.

During the inter-war years the association of Jews with the East End held fast, though social mobility was already claiming the exit of hundreds to the new environs: east to the suburbs of Ilford, north to Clapton and Stamford Hill, and for the more affluent, Golders Green in the north-west, along the road towards integration and, for the majority, eventual *embourgeoisement*. The Second World War proved a watershed, which spelt finis to Jewish East London. Hitler's *Luftwaffe* and greater opportunities in a more affluent society have opened wide the old walls, and the Children of the Ghetto have fled. Since the 1950s the last bastions of the *shtetl* have crumbled, with Zangwillian Whitechapel already a legend, as its old bounds are transmogrified into Indian or Bangla-Deshi settlements.

Today a few mumbling ancients still shuffle their way through the new 'alien' streets towards the odd, surviving *stiebel*, eager to sustain a *minyan* (a quorum of ten adult males needed to hold a service). Here, in the empty *shools*, they commune with ghosts, the past depositors of the ghetto's sadness and glory. The old

Yiddish poet Avram Stencl slowly paces the White-chapel Waste, lamenting the going of his people, yet still writing of and for them. For to him the present *is* the past. He breathes continuity, as timeless as the *bagel* boobas of the Lane, the salt and pickle herring vendors of Old Montague Street, the warm, noisy, *heimischkeit* of *Bloom's*.

What, in retrospect, did the Jewish immigrants contribute to the host community? Were they during their whole term of settlement a threat or an asset? Certain definitive answers emerge:

(a) They developed a new industry—cheap clothing—to meet the demand of an increasing working class and lower middle class market. In the process they did *not* deprive local Englishmen of labour; on the contrary, they expanded employment in the tailoring trade, especially among women.

(b) They brought with them a commercial and business acumen which eventually fulfilled itself in the milieu of freedom, although these so-called qualities were imposed on them by Russian discrimination as well as historical limitations of employment in the Christian world.

(c) A second generation of artists, philosophers, teachers, musicians, doctors and lawyers emerged, in which scholarship was inbred, derived from the traditional compulsory reading of the Talmud that geared the young to early study and intellectual discourse. In the ghetto slums a thousand flowers bloomed (among whom were Mark Gertler (artist), Isaac Rosenberg (poet and artist), writers and playwrights Israel Zangwill and Arnold Wesker, scientists and philosophers Selig Brodetsky and Jacob Bronowski).

(d) A sense of social justice, derived from their own suffering, which they translated into political action. Many joined the labour movement and rendered pioneer and selfless service to their cause, e.g. Mannie Shinwell (Labour Minister), J. L. Fine (Trade Union leader), Phil Piratin (Communist MP). Among the leadership and rank-and-file the immigrants and their children fought for the dispossessed.

Integration being now complete, what can we learn from the Jewish story? At the least, just as their experience as victims developed into a sympathetic identification with the oppressed poor elsewhere, so may we come to recognise that divisions of race and creed are of little significance in our own appreciation of strangers within the gates.

But, to date, this message seems neither to be received nor understood! For, with the coming of the Commonwealth immigrants, patterns of settlement (and host reaction) comparable to their Jewish predecessors are detected; although, by contrast, in the three years 1955–7 the influx of coloured immigrants (132,000) had already surpassed the grand total of Jews who came over a span of forty years.

In the early post-war period colonial migration into the East End was mainly from West Africa. In the numbers game it was minuscule. By 1950, it was 145 and the 1951 census confirmed this (*see Banton*). By 1961 the total African population of Stepney was 598. As the majority were concentrated in the area between the Commercial Road and the London Docks (especially along Cable Street) there was some growth of anti-coloured sentiment in the vicinity. The proliferation of 'café society' with its concomitant expansion of clubs and brothels in the St. George's precincts prompted magistrate and club leader Basil Henriques to complain of an invasion of an 'army of prostitutes' who were pestering the coloureds (*East End News*, 19 November 1954). His main attack was against the Colonial Office who had failed to provide hostel accommodation, with the result that the black immigrants 'have nothing to do but haunt the cafés'. This, partially valid, criticism, taken up by less reputable interests, was symptomatic of a growing anti-alien reaction at grass roots. It was the rapid intake of Indians and Pakistanis in the late 1950s and early 1960s that fanned the embers of resentment. An economic recession, when it came, would provide the opportunity for the racists to project themselves, convincingly, as sole defenders of British homes and jobs against the alien 'predator'.

As with the Jews, chain migration with frequent reinforcements from the homelands aided by relatively cheaper air travel brought colour into national prominence. Locally, quarters recently evacuated by the Jews were rapidly filled up by the newcomers, the largest concentration by 1961 being in the Spitalfields, Whitechapel and neighbouring wards. Since then they

In Mile End Road

have, in repeat performance of the Jewish act but with less spectacular numbers, flowed over the borders into the neighbouring streets of Mile End and St. George's.

It was the old pattern repeated. The legendary London, streets paved with gold, was the magnet for a poor, rural folk, desperately seeking escape from perennial disaster—where floods brought homelessness and hunger and civil strife spelt mass murder. The East End was relatively tolerant. It had contained the Jews, nurtured them and sent them forth strengthened to new pastures. With its diminishing population and a still flourishing light engineering industry, chemical

and transport plants, labour was in short supply. Above all, there was the traditional clothing trade, its continuity sustained from Huguenot to Jew. It was not long before the small Jewish manufacturer and domestic outworker was first reinforced, and then replaced, by his immigrant successor. Zangwill's ghetto is gone. But in the side streets of Brick Lane—Fournier Street, Wilkes Street, Princelet Street and Hanbury Street—can still be heard the endless hum and whirl of tailors' machines, just as it was when the great Jewish chronicler walked these same streets a century ago.

Jewish Bakery, Quaker Streeet

Trading in Hessel Street

In the imagination, as in reality, the small, thin figures, skull-capped and ill at ease in their dark Western suits, forming a garrulous chattering ensemble on the side walks or quietly plodding on their way in pairs or groups, a gentle people, starkly convey to the discerning onlooker a sort of reincarnation of the lost world of the Yiddish 'greener'. Only the colour of their skin betrays them. The corner shop, the all-purpose store is still there—under new management. *Halal* butchers, where a Muslim *kashrut* strictly prevails, signify their existence in Bengali instead of Hebrew. The *Machzikei Hadath* is now the Great Mosque (*Jamme Masjid*) packed to overflowing at Ramadan as it was yesteryear on Yom Kippur. The family remains sacrosanct, as do their ancient religion and culture—a bastion of defensive orthodoxy in the midst of a hostile society.

It was the old Adam—sex—and the growing incidence of prostitution that resuscitated immigration as an issue, although this had little to do with the Asian community whose religious *mores* (like the Jews') imposed strict standards of private and public morality. Evidence suggests that merchants of vice were more likely to be found among the Maltese, Somalis or de-culturised West Indians, though not exclusively so. A Stepney campaign against 'physical and moral dirt' underwent two stages. The first (1957–8) paralleled the race riots in Notting Hill and Nottingham, but the organisers (particularly the Communist Party group) were careful not to identify Maltese or black, as such, except where unavoidable, in order to encourage participation by coloured residents themselves. But leaders of the second campaign (1960–1), in tune with populist prejudice, were ready to define the problem as an immigrant one. Local anti-vice propagandist Father Williamson wrote (*pp. 135–6*): 'The situation has been made far worse by the numbers of coloured people who have moved into the area . . . it is a fact that most of the bad cafés and clubs that have been opened in the area in the past few years are owned by Maltese, Somalis, Cypriots, West Indians and other immigrants.' Such accusations provided ammunition for the protagonists of immigrant control, which had by then become the subject of national

Former East End synagogue, now a dress factory, 1978

Chevrah Shass synagogue, 1972, now demolished

Synagogue in Princelet Street

debate. In July 1962 a new Immigration Act became law. Extreme nationalists and racist parties had successfully projected their issue, which henceforth grew from strength to strength, not least in the festering corners of East London.

With further legal restrictions and immigration acts, anti-alien sentiment has not abated. On the contrary, with the present economic recession, numbers need not necessarily define the issue, while the sacrificial lamb is still available to the high priests of racism and exclusion. In autumn 1969 violence erupted in the streets as roving gangs of young thugs (self-styled skin-heads) went on the rampage beating up Pakistanis, culminating in a minor pogrom in the Spitalfields area by early 1970 with one poor Asian kitchen porter being stabbed to death. (The West Indians were *not* the target, possibly because they appear to be accepted as 'black' Englishmen, but more likely because they are able to fight back very effectively when attacked, in contrast to the more 'timid' Asians.) With the growth of the National Front, working (as the Mosleyites and the British Brothers' League did before them) on the primitive fears and prejudices of discontented locals, threats to the security of the Bengla-Deshi community have become more potent—more so as the NF, partly due to their continual exposure by the media, assume the respectability of a *bona fide* political party.

93

'Though all things differ, all agree.' Like the Jews, they were at first difficult to unionise for fear of offending their own, immigrant, employer and the need to work all hours to maximise their earnings, since the money accrued must needs meet the cost of maintaining their poor kinsfolk back home or help pay their passage to Britain. The *East London Advertiser*, which at the turn of the century was lamenting the inflictions brought on East London by the 'pauper foreigners', in 1972 reported like reactions by its modern contributors, in headlines curiously unchanged: *Immigrants blamed for 'slave conditions'; Ragtrade 'sweatshops' scandal; Child 'slaves' in sweat shops row.* As of yore, housing shortage brought on the accusation that Bengalis were monopolising living

Tailor's sign, Princelet Street

Graffiti, Bethnal Green Road

accommodation. In the local press complaints proliferated. 'I fail to see any homeless immigrants', wrote
one angry reader. Another: 'As regards housing, every
house, flat or room taken by an immigrant means one
less for an English person born and bred here.' Of
course there was no real evidence to justify these
pronouncements. In fact the immigrants had the least
chance of acquiring adequate modern accommodation,
and were thereby forced into the oldest, barely
habitable houses. That their options were limited to
those very houses and streets once exclusive to Jews
confirms this. And with space at a premium, overcrowding was inevitable.

The newcomers continue to be accused of the same
offences as their predecessors: of clannishness— that
is, deliberate separatism—although, on their part, the
local host community have made little attempt to
encourage social integration; of Bengalis indulging in
'unhygienic habits'—'They block up the drains with
their rubbish' and are therefore carriers of disease
(racists suggest that the immigrants import foul
diseases, such as leprosy and syphilis, to undermine
the white race); of their children overrunning local
schools, resulting in the exclusion of Christian children
and a deterioration in educational standards. The
attacks persist—*in toto* a combination of irrational
prejudice and deliberate ploy on the part of political
opportunists—bearing their evil fruit in a receptive
climate which, conjuring up scapegoats like circuses,
diverts attention from the real issues. Yesterday it was
the Jews, today the coloureds.

Perhaps we may leave the last words to Caroline
Adams, who has successfully undertaken pioneer
work in community relations among the Bengalis in
East London. In her pamphlet 'They sell cheaper and
they live very odd' (1977) she perceptively compares
and contrasts the Jewish and Bengali experience vis à
vis the host community.

The reactions of the Bengali Community, particularly its
youth, to these verbal attacks, and to the vicious physical
assaults which have accompanied them, and the con-
sequent developments within the community, indicate
that the Bengali East End will eventually claim as
important a place in British history as the Jewish East End
has claimed, and that history will leave its detractors as
foolish as do those of the Jews.

In Sheba Street, off Quaker Street

95

Former synagogue in Christian Street

In Settles Street

Wholesale warehouse off Brick Lane

Raj & Sons factory, Bethnal Green Road

The *Jack the Ripper*, Commercial Street

CRIME

In the 1880s East London was already an over-pressurised ghetto of immigrants and internal and external displaced labour, where the perimeters of poverty and hunger were rapidly expanding. The pressure gauge was ready to burst.

At climactic periods of unemployment and social unrest it did. In the East End milieu outbursts manifested themselves in two distinctive patterns—by a peak crime wave and by a radical upsurge—mainly separate responses to the same stimuli—but, in one major incident, a fusion of the two. This was the Sidney Street Siege (1911), the second great horror legend which achieved international fame.

The first was the infamous Whitechapel murders of 1888, performed by that ubiquitous gentleman of the night, Jack the Ripper. For East Enders and beyond he still remains one of the two folk 'heroes' of their locale. Had his identity been discovered and had he been brought to trial, his exploits would merely have registered another sordid tale of a murderer brought to justice such as that of wife-dismemberer Dr Crippen and the Boston strangler. But he was never caught. His identity remains the greatest enigma in the annals of unsolved crime.

The unlit cobbled alleyways, harbingers of patrolling ladies of the night, provided an ideal setting for murder by an insane killer. (The Whitechapel Board of Works were debating the extension of gas lamps into the ill-lit alleyways of Spitalfields just before the Ripper struck.) In the early hours of a hot summer morning, 7 August 1888, a policeman was passing an arched dark alley along the Whitechapel Road—George Yard (now Gunthorpe Street, it is still there just as it was!)—when he was confronted by an agitated

The *Jack the Ripper*, detail

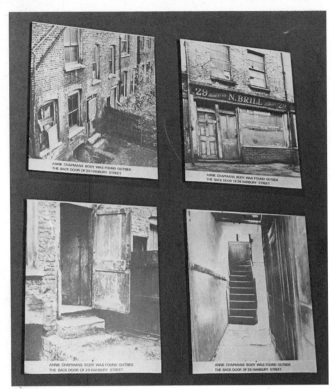

Inside the *Jack the Ripper*, scenes of the third
Ripper murder, 29 Hanbury Street

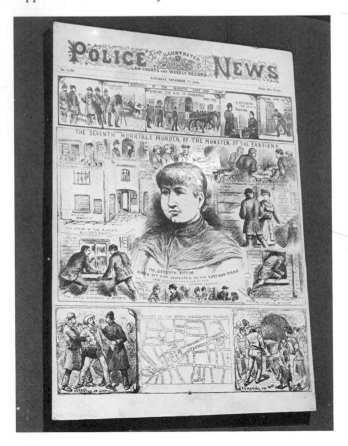

market porter who had stumbled over the corpse of a woman. Making their way along the alley to the George Yard Buildings near the St. Jude's vicarage, they found the woman spreadeagled on the first-floor steps. On closer examination the constable was horrified. The body resembled a human pepper pot, the torso bloody with the cuts of innumerable knife wounds. The victim was soon identified as Martha Turner, a local street walker of the cheapest type. (It is still debated whether Turner was the first victim. Some 'Ripperologists' suggest that Polly Nichols was the first. From the nature and ferocity of the attacks one could conclude that they were carried out by the same killer.) A second body, that of 'Polly' Nichols, was found early on Saturday morning, 31 August, half-a-mile away at Bucks Row. (Now the desolate Durward Street. The corpse was found near what is now S. Rosenberger, Coates & Co. Ltd.) Her body had suffered terrible mutilations. A wave of terror and hysteria was sparked off in the East End, as four more victims fell to the knife—all prostitutes, always at night—during an eight-week spread lasting till November. The last victim, Mary Jane Kelly, was found to have been despatched particularly brutally, her body skilfully dismantled and her innards strung across the room like Christmas decorations. Later murders were preceded by letters to the Press, under the signature of Jack the Ripper, in which the murderer brazenly outlined his intent. Scotland Yard's inability to stop the Ripper bemused Londoners and puzzled the world press. Sir Melville Macnaughton, Head of the Yard, long after recalled: 'No one who was living in London that Autumn will forget the terror. Even now I remember the foggy evenings and the newspaper boys shouting, "Another murder in Whitechapel, murder, murder, murder!".' There were few clues and rumour was rife. The Ripper was believed to be a man, though some deduced that it could be a woman, perhaps a midwife, who had some knowledge of anatomy and could have explained away her presence in the streets at night in bloodstained clothing. Unverified reports came of a heavy dark-cloaked gentleman with a top hat prowling through the fog, others declaring that he wore a deerstalker. The latter headgear would help effect an important literary creation.

Views on his identity continued, and still continue, to be speculative: one that he was a doctor or medical student from the famous local London Hospital; another that he was a Jewish immigrant, which led to

Inside the *Jack the Ripper*, contemporary newspaper

43 Durward Street, approximate scene of the second Ripper murder today

a minor pogrom, with local Jews being beaten up in the street (see above pp. 84–5; the fourth victim, Elizabeth Stride, was found outside the predominantly Jewish Working Men's Educational Club in Berner Street). Most bizarre of all, at the time, was the conviction that he was a slaughter-house worker (*see Law (1), pp. 208 ff.*). Police enquiries revealed that several men quit their jobs at the time of the murders. Two were traced to the USA—one to Chicago, the other to Kansas City. Pinkerton agents actually commissioned by Scotland Yard caught up with them, questioned both thoroughly, and vindicated them. There was also suspicion of evil in high places, which fell on the young Duke of Clarence, a noted eccentric, fond of deerstalker

hats and prone to strange nocturnal wanderings. The evidence is, to say the least, inconclusive. More convincing is the theory, recently proffered by author Dan Farson, that the Ripper was one Montague Druitt, crazy lawyer-cum-schoolmaster, a Wykehamist and frequent visitor to his brother Dr Lionel Druitt who lodged in Whitechapel. His body was fished out of the Thames in December just after the murders had ceased abruptly.

Horror stories aside, the murders resulted in some long-term assets. The miserable victims proved sacrificial in determining at least three important derivatives. The first was aid in the creation of the most famous detective in international fiction. It was

103

Scotland Yard's failure to catch the Ripper that prompted Dr Arthur Conan Doyle to conjure up a super-sleuth who could: ironically building the physical image of Sherlock Holmes on that of society's elusive quarry—cloak, cane, deerstalker hat and all. It is significant that many of the tales are set against the fog-ridden alleyways and dens of Whitechapel. Second was the heightening of the Victorian social conscience, finally aroused to the plight of outcast London which the Ripper publicity revealed.

National and international attention was then focused on the East End. It was reflected in two ways. First in the renewed concentration of effort to alleviate the terrible incidence of homeless and abandoned children—a running sore of the metropolis. Their role as perpetual recruits to criminal gangs had been underlined by Dickens in his earlier novels, such as *Oliver Twist*, with the sinister *procureurs* Fagin and Bill Sykes operating in the peripheral parishes of the East End. As we have seen (pp. 50–4 above), Dr Barnardo had pioneered the movement to rescue homeless and pauper children, and the process was aided by the revelation of the social background to the Whitechapel murders: accelerated perhaps, but still inadequate to meet the need. In 1896, Arthur Morrison, ex-Civil Servant and student of the London underworld, could pile horror upon horror in his *Child of the Jago*, a novel of poverty and crime based on Shoreditch. The young 'hero' is early initiated into the philosophy of the slum dweller. An old lag points out to him the tough ruthless mobsters who rule the precinct and the need to emulate them:

> 'There it is—that's your aim in life—there's your pattern. Learn to read and write, learn all you can; but learn cunning, spare nobody and stop at nothing. It's the best this world has for you, For the Jago's got you, and it's the only way out, except the gaol and the gallows!'

The Jago, one of the foulest of East End rookeries, swarmed with young thugs of the calibre of Dicky Perrott. The father, ex-plasterer, feckless and work-less, carries a cosh, and his family exists on what he can plunder from his victims. No stranger ventures into the heart of the Jago, unless he is drunk. No law is enforced there, the police enter singly at their peril, so the normal invasion by the law is in large posses. Gang wars rage up and down the foul and noisome courts, the police being forced to intervene only when someone is killed. The denizens of the Jago have an

Nineteenth-century mug shots

ingrained conviction that it is the respectable citizen who is wrong, not they, on the precept that 'YOU are wrong in the first place for appropriating all the good things the world affords, leaving for them but what they steal; and . . . they regard all *your* endeavours to persuade them to abandon the wretched life of thief for the equally poor though more creditable existence of an honest lad as humbug and selfishness . . . They believe the clergy are all hypocrites, the judges and magistrates tyrants, and honest people their bitterest enemies!' Considering the smug Victorian preachings on the virtue of laissez faire and self-help, they had a good case. For their grim outlook is still the *credo* of a minority of East Enders, nursed in the family tradition of crime, who likewise satisfy their own acquisitive urges in a free, competitive market!

The second response was a vigorous programme for rehousing the local poor, prompted as much by the need to sweep away the festering centres of danger to society, as the desire to alleviate the conditions of the 'lower classes'. Finally, it was no doubt social

No. 94. Mary Jones
Street thief
32 old.
5ft high
dark hair
hazel eyes
fresh comp
15 mo. C.C. May 1870

other convictions

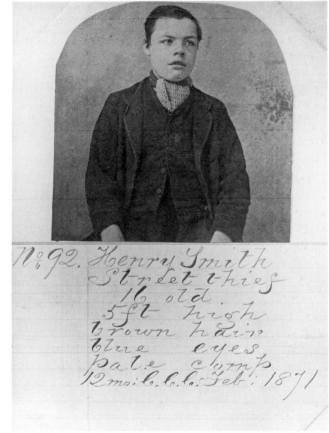

No. 92. Henry Smith
Street thief
16 old
5ft high
brown hair
blue eyes
pale comp
12 mo. C.C. Feb. 1871

expediency as well as social conscience that engendered the first professional study of an urban poor area to be conducted in the East End. In that same terrible year, 1888, in that same Gunthorpe Street, where 'Jack' had operated on his first victim, Charles Booth, industrialist and pioneer sociologist, set up headquarters for his research team to extend a local preliminary survey (*Booth, C. (3), pp. 326–91*) into the monumental *Life and Labour of the People of London*, which was later published (1892–7). It is still the great classic study of the labouring poor in the social sciences. Social investigators have, till recently, maintained the tradition of research based on the East End, the fountainhead of modern case studies.

In an area of ceaseless deprivation petty crime was a positive necessity. 'It's steal or ring the workhouse bell' pleaded the poor. If caught, better warm cell than the cold Bastille. For police and thief alike the area continued to provide a laboratory for criminal innovation. There were gradations of thievery. The lowest was *kynchin lay*—stealing from children,

especially when delivering laundry for their mothers, whose only income might be derived from 'taking in washing'—or the *mutcher*, a predator who stole from drunks. *Shootflying*, gold watch-chain snatching, was a common pursuit, and *whizzers*, pickpockets, abounded in the street markets and crowded thoroughfares. A busy craftsman was the counterfeiter with his aide, the *smasher* (passer of false money), although this turned out to be a precarious occupation. There was always a *nose* (informer) around, and rare is the tale of coiner escaping justice. Among minor aberrations was the continuing tradition of large-scale pilfering on the job, particularly in the docks, where perks included tobacco leaves, butter, liquor and any other commodities 'won' during onloading. Over all there developed sophisticated means of depriving the more affluent of their 'surplus' money or belongings: burglary being a specialist 'trade' passed on from generation to generation. Such continuity might be expected in an area constantly peopled by low-income groups, where unemployment and housing problems are still rife, so that, in some families, crime has become a hereditary way of life. (I can recall examples of these from my own youth in Stepney, and later in my early days as a local schoolmaster teaching youngsters whose families followed the hereditary occupation of house burglars! W.J.F.).

In such a milieu gangs flourished. They lived by terrorism and blackmail, drawing their recruits from the lodging houses that were spawned during the late Victorian and Edwardian eras. They extorted 'protection' money from keepers of shabby restaurants and pubs (both pick-up centres for prostitutes), runners of gambling dens, street bookies and 'straight' shopkeepers. Fights broke out over protection territories between mobsters armed with knives and revolvers, but prosecutions were difficult to sustain since witnesses were too scared to give evidence.

In East London, as in New York, even the law-abiding immigrants were not free from home-bred gangsterdom. At the turn of the century, the protection racket was worked by a powerful mob, numbering up to forty Russians, the self-styled Bessarabian Tigers who preyed mainly on fellow Jews, who, in turn, were too intimidated to inform the police. A turning point came when a group of them was sent to demand money of a Jewish shopkeeper Kikal. He refused to pay and seizing an axe sent them flying for their lives. Inspired by his example, the long-suffering victims banded themselves together to select and set up a vigilante group for common protection. Within a few weeks the new caucus under the name of the Odessians were themselves demanding money with threats. Both gangs continued to pursue a programme of robbery, extortion and mayhem for many years. In two of their escapades, at least, they achieved widespread notoriety.

In 1902 a Russian police officer holidaying in London was waylaid, robbed and badly beaten up, while visiting in the East End. A description of the assailants tallied with those of three Bessarabian ringleaders: Max Moses (known as Kid McCoy!), a first-class boxer with championship pretensions, Barnet Brozishewski and Joseph Weinstein. They were seized by the police, charged with highway robbery and violence and slapped into custody. During their one week on remand, the Russian officer received a note warning him that if he gave evidence the only prospect of his returning to his native land would be in a coffin. 'Deciding that discretion was the better part of

valour he departed incontinently to spend the rest of his holiday in his own land' (*Wensley, pp. 107–8*). The result—McCoy was sentenced to a mere fine, and his henchmen discharged under notice of re-arrest if evidence was forthcoming. It never came.

Two months later (October 1902) the Bessarabians learned that their Odessian rivals were engaged en bloc in a drinking session at the *York Minster* pub in Philpot Street. Silently mobilising outside they made a sudden attack on the packed house, viciously laying about them with cudgels and knives. One Odessian, Brodovitch, was stabbed to death, and the police, called quickly to the affray, seized gang leader Brozishewski on the spot. Other Bessarabian leaders, McCoy and Samuel Oreman, who had been seen wielding weapons at the time, were soon tracked down and arrested. All three were committed for trial and found guilty of manslaughter: McCoy received 10 years' and Oreman 5 years' penal servitude, the more fortunate Brozishewski only six months' hard labour. This resulted in a short-term recession in gang warfare, without any notable decline in gang strength.

Violence peaked during the long winter of 1910–11. The 'Aldgate mob', led by one M. Bogard (nicknamed Darkie the Coon because of his sallow complexion, his face also resembling the cross lines of a railway complex as a result of razor slashing), was constantly in gang fights over 'territory'. In March 1911 such incidents reached a climax after an inter-gang fight broke out on the steps of the Worship Street Court during the hearing of a *vendetta* case involving a knife attack on Darkie the Coon and his mob. The police actually found themselves powerless to control the fracas, which turned into a battle as more and more villains joined in on the opposing sides. (A comprehensive study of East End crime during this period is recorded in Raphael Samuel's forthcoming book *East End Underworld, 1887–1947*.) In a climate of violence and mayhem, murder was, naturally, not uncommon.

At 2.30 a.m. on 15 March 1909, the body of William Sproull, second engineer of the steamer *Dorset* currently berthed in the Victoria Docks, was found in Rupert Street, just round the corner from Leman Street police station. He had been stabbed to death. Quick action on the part of the police revealed that he had been enticed by two girls to No. 3 Rupert Street. This was verified by a trail of bloodstains and threepenny pieces leading to that house, and on the very panels of the door was a bloodstained impression of a man's right hand. Two tenants of this lodging house were well known to the police—the brothers Marks and Moses Reubens, both ponces (i.e. men living on the earnings of prostitutes) and previously suspected of robbery with violence.

That same morning the police entered and seized Marks. In room No. 13 they found a girl in a drunken sleep, who, when sobered up, agreed that she had brought a man there the night before. Brother Moses was discovered ensconced with a prostitute in a room on the first floor. Interrogated on the spot, he admitted to having fought the deceased but only to defend himself from a drunken attack, but under sharper questioning he confessed to having robbed the man as he lay unconscious, adding, 'I hope he is not dead'. The victim's watch and chain was found suspended on a hook sewn inside a leg of trousers belonging to Moses. When informed that the man had died of knife wounds, he wept and pleaded his innocence, declaring 'If he was stabbed, my brother must have stabbed him!' The murder weapon was found hidden behind the gas stove of his own room. Brought to trial at the Old Bailey, the Reubens case made headlines. The brothers were both found guilty of murder and executed on 24 May 1909. According to the (later) Chief Constable Wensley: 'From that date robbery with violence became unfashionable in East London and few unaccountable dead bodies were found in the streets.'

However, 1911 marked the launching of the second greatest crime legend in East End folk lore. On 17 December 1910 London awoke to the news of a triple murder of policemen in a cul-de-sac at the back of a jeweller's shop in Houndsditch. (Proprietor H. S. Harris at 119 Houndsditch. His son Harry was still operating the business in 1945.) It appeared that a neighbouring employee, Mr Max Weil, had become alarmed at non-stop banging at the rear of the shop late at night, and notified a P.C. Piper, stationed at Bishopsgate. On investigating a ground-floor flat at No. 11 Exchange Buildings in Cutler Street, whose walls adjoined those of the jeweller, the constable had his suspicions aroused by the furtive behaviour of the 'foreigner' who opened the door, and he summoned the assistance of five other policemen led by a Sergeant Bentley. As they entered the premises they were greeted with a burst of gunfire. The gang leader, seized by a P.C. Choat, was mortally wounded by the bullets fired by his comrades to dislodge his captor. Choat and

Cutler Street from Exchange Buildings. Scene of the Houndsditch murders, 1911

two others lay dead as two men and a girl carried their dying accomplice through the side streets of White-chapel to their destination at 59 Grove Street, off the Commercial Road.

There, on a bed in a small back room, he spent his last hours. Two women remained to minister to him—Sara Rosa Trassjonsky and Luba Milstein. In desperation, and in defiance of strict orders left by the rest of the gang who had quit, Rosa called on a local Dr Scanlon, who soon caught on to the situation, and notified the police. The news broke with a police description in all papers of four men, including the dead one, who was quickly identified as George

Gardstein, alias Poolka Kilkowitz, alias Muronzeff, who for some months had occupied a room at 44 Gold Street, Stepney Green. It appeared self-evident that there was some connection with the local Anarchist group, since in Rosa's flat were copies of the *Arbeter Fraint* and *Germinal* as well as similar Russian and Yiddish publications underneath the dead man's pillow. The hunt was on for the remaining three: Peter the Painter or Peter Piatkov, alias Schtern (regarded as the brains behind the robbery), Fritz Svaas and the last, later identified as the limping man, Joseph Marx.

Hardly had the hue and cry after Houndsditch begun to subside when the second drama broke. On 2 January 1911, a Mrs Gershon, living at 100 Sidney Street (a house located about fifty yards from, and parallel to, the Anarchist Club) arrived at Arbour Square police station to report that two men, who had rented a room from her on the first floor, answered to the descriptions on the 'wanted' posters. The police surrounded the house and the tragi-comedy began. The men, sensing that they had been betrayed, seized their landlady and deprived her of her skirt and boots on the assumption that no religious Jewess would attempt to make a break in her underclothes. But Mrs Gershon was made of sterner stuff, and slid out while her captors' backs were turned. This set the scene for the first act in the affair of Sidney Street.

At seven-thirty next morning a policeman threw gravel at the first-floor window. There was a burst of gunfire, and a police Sergeant Leeson, posted opposite by the brewery wall, fell wounded in the chest. A gun battle ensued between police and desperadoes which continued for over two hours. At ten a.m., after an appeal to the Tower Garrison, a force of two squads of Scots Guards in battle regalia was brought up as reinforcements. A barrage of cross-fire was directed at the floor, where the besieged had erected a barricade of bedding and furniture across the windows. Meanwhile the Home Secretary, Winston Churchill, had arrived on the scene ostensibly to direct operations. By lunch-time a whiff of smoke emerged from one of the windows on the first floor, and the return fire ceased abruptly. The house was soon immersed in flames. It is still an open question whether one survivor had set fire to it rather than surrender or whether it had been started by an incendiary device thrown from outside. When the firemen had finished (after five of them had been injured by falling masonry), two charred bodies were found and identified as those of Svaas and Marx.

Peter Piatkov (Peter the Painter). Police photograph, *c.* 1910

It was deduced that Marx died first since he had a bullet in the brain, while Svaas might have succumbed to suffocation after having started the fire. But the main police target, Peter the Painter, vanished; and so was born East London's second legendary anti-hero.

The happenings at Houndsditch and Sidney Street overshadowed an equally bizarre case of homicide. It concerned the discovery of the body of an immigrant dealer and slum property owner Louis Beron on Clapham Common in the early hours of New Year's day (1911). He had been battered to death, and a curious *S* sign scratched on his forehead. (This mark *S* (Russian—*Spion* for spy) provoked one belief that he

The Siege of Sidney Street, 1912

might have been a Russian secret police agent and therefore his murder was an act of vengeance by unknown Russian revolutionaries.) Suspicion fell on ex-con. Steinie Morrison (his real name was Morris Stern) who before 1910 held a twelve-year record as burglar and thief, having chosen this career at the age of 17. He had been released on licence on 17 September 1910, and subsequently worked for a short time as a baker's assistant in Lavender Hill, less than ten minutes' walk from the murder spot. Police evidence, some of which is still considered dubious, suggested that he was the last to see the victim alive: first, he had been observed conversing with Beron late at night on 31 December; secondly—clinching evidence—cabbies claimed that they recognised him as the man who accompanied Beron in their carriage en route to Clapham. The trial proved sensational, as much because of the sympathy evoked by the bearing of the prisoner as because of the antics of defence counsel. He was found guilty, but the death sentence was commuted, on appeal, by the Home Secretary, Winston Churchill, to life imprisonment. The prisoner passionately denied his guilt to the end, and the case of Steinie Morrison is, to this day, the subject of legal debate.

The post-1945 years have seen the East End relieved of its nineteenth-century image of crime and mayhem together with its traditional definition as 'the City of Dreadful Night'. Social and economic improvements have no doubt contributed to its 'moral' improvement, although a universal relative affluence and materialistic *mores* have not progressively reduced the overall crime rate.

It may be that old habits die hard and the gangs continued to operate. Responding to sound economic precepts, London post-war crime bosses embarked on schemes, sometimes voluntarily enforced, of vertical and horizontal integration. Territories were still defined and defended against incursions by rival predators, but gangs continued to limit their perimeters by mutual consent. At first the East End patch was dominated by club owner Jack 'Spot' Comer, an ambitious muscle man, who first collaborated with the legendary mobster Billy Hill, boss of the West End underworld. Overriding caution, at one point Spot reckoned he was ready to replace Hill and annex his domain. He quickly suffered a set-back, but as Charles Kray drily records:

A ferocious striping at the hands (and razor) of 'Mad' Frankie Fraser did nothing to cool his ambitions. After the surgeons had sewed his face together he continued to prove that he was stupid as well as brainless by carrying on his attempts to topple Billy from his throne. His activities were brought to an abrupt conclusion by the attentions of one Albert Dimes (born Alberto Dimeo) who chased the luckless Spot down a Soho side-street and gave him a proper seeing-to before a crowd of witnesses who were later found to be dumb and blind.

Whether the none-too-gentle dissuasion of Mr Comer was performed at the instigation of Billy Hill I do not know, nor do I care to hazard a guess. Mr Comer changed his name to Mr Colmore and, according to my latest information, subject to confirmation, is utilising his inconsiderable talents in packing a well-known brand of sausages into suitable containers at a factory in Park Royal.

(*Kray, p. 100*)

It was the shooting of George Cornell by Ronald Kray in the bar of the *Blind Beggar*, Whitechapel, on the evening of 6 March 1966, that finally exposed the activities of the Kray brothers to both national and international publicity. By their exploits the East End has acquired a third legend in its tradition of anti-heroes. The story of their rise and fall has become a growth industry and can be read elsewhere. Their original contribution to the nature of East End crime was, perhaps, threefold. They were the first of the local breed who were not drawn to commit crimes through need or childhood insecurity. On the contrary theirs was a relatively comfortable background with a close family commitment. Secondly, their empire spread beyond the boundaries of the home base. Chicago-style racketeerism of the 1920s plus an effective strong-arm intelligence extended the Krays' power across London into the provinces. Before their fall, the Bethnal Green lads were riding high. (They were seriously exploring a link-up with a US 'Syndicate' when Detective-Superintendent 'Nipper' Read struck!) Thirdly, there was the Robin Hood image that they still project, particularly among the local poor, who were recipients of the many charities they promoted, and of their many acts of personal generosity. On the Krays' part 'Charitable activities were good for the image—and it wasn't all that unpleasant to lash out a few quid for the benefit of old people and kids and, in general, do something in a practical way to help those who had not been so fortunate as us'—although 'there was no adverse comment from the nurses at Mile End hospital, the Queen Elizabeth Hospital for Children, the Cancer Campaign appeals, the Repton Boys' Club and other organisations which benefited from our fund raising efforts' (*Kray, pp. 134–5*).

In all, the sensational and the horrific, once the hallmarks of our local saga, are hollow resonances of the past. Today the streets of East London offer free and open passage to native and stranger alike. Yet in the imagination is the true reality. Even now, in the still hours, as the moon strikes the steeple of old Christ Church, and casts a long shadow over the rickety tenements of Spitalfields, a sudden catch of movement, crouched silhouette in a desolate alleyway, all senses alert, as Old Jack, poised momentarily en route, continues on his way to a rendezvous with murder in the City of Dreadful Night.

Sidney Street, surviving corner

The *Blind Beggar*, where George Cornell was shot by Ronald Kray

Graffito protesting the innocence of the convicted criminal George Davis

Annie Besant (1847–1933)

RADICALS

In May 1975 the first National Museum of Labour History was opened by Prime Minister Harold Wilson at the Limehouse Town Hall. It was a fitting location. Within a square mile of that building were enacted some of the greatest dramas in the saga of working-class liberation.

Significantly the traumatic year 1888 was also the *annus mirabilis* in the making of organised labour. It saw the birth of the New Unionism pioneered by a woman for women—the most exploited sector of the community. She was Annie Besant (1847–1933).

An ardent feminist, she had quit her authoritarian husband, the Rev. Frank Besant, in 1873, subsequently losing custody of her eight-year-old daughter under a Court of Chancery ruling that she was unfit to act as guardian because of her advocacy of atheism and contraception. After 1874, in partnership with Charles Bradlaugh, she campaigned for secularism; and for publishing birth-control pamphlets they were both hauled before the Queen's Bench in the famous trial of 1877. Her radical commitment drew her, through Fabianism, into the ranks of the Social-Democratic Federation (1885) when she contributed articles to *Justice*. The confrontation of 'Bloody Sunday' (13 November 1887, when a peaceful meeting of the unemployed in Trafalgar Square was violently broken up by police action) helped sharpen her activism, and, in retrospect, heightened her quest for a 'new Church dedicated to the teaching of social duty, the upholding of social righteousness, the building of a true commonwealth'. Such ideas accorded with those of radical journalist W. T. Stead, so together in January 1888 they launched a new ½d. weekly, the *Link*, with a fanfare of rhetoric. ('The People are Silent . . . I will be the WORD of the People. I will be the bleeding mouth whence the gag is snatched out. I will say everything!')

Exposure of the terrible exploitation of women in this short-lived journal sparked off the historic strike of the match girls at Bow. During a meeting of the Fabian Society (15 June 1888) devoted to a lecture by Clementina Black and discussion on female labour, H. H. Champion 'drew attention to the wages paid by Bryant and May (Ltd.) while paying an enormous dividend to their shareholders so that the value of the original £5 shares was quoted at £18.7.6d.' (*Besant, p. 334*). As a follow-up, Annie Besant interviewed some girl employees to attain a list of their piece rates and charges. Horrified at her findings, she published the article 'White Slavery in London' in the *Link* (23 June) attacking Bryant and May and calling for a boycott of their product. On 26 June she and her companion, Herbert Burrows, distributed the article to the match girls as they came out of the factory gates.

An immediate response was a threat of libel action by the company against Besant and a demand by management that the workers refute the charges by signing a paper certifying that they were well treated and that the accusations were untrue. They refused and a girl marked out as their leader was dismissed. On 5 July, 672 women downed tools and quit the factory. The East End rallied to their aid. Under Besant and Burrows a strike committee was formed and a national appeal for funds brought money pouring in from a mass of sympathisers. Besant records:

We registered the girls to receive strike pay, wrote articles, roused the clubs, held public meetings, got Mr Bradlaugh to ask questions in Parliament, stirred up

Match girls' strike, 1888

constituencies in which shareholders were members, till the whole country rang with the struggle. Mr Frederick Charrington lent us a hall for registration, Mr Sidney Webb and others moved the National Liberal Club to action; we led a procession of the girls to the House of Commons, and interviewed, with a deputation of them, Members of Parliament who cross-questioned them . . . Mr Hobart of the Social Democratic Federation, Messrs Shaw, Bland and Oliver and Headlam of the Fabian Society, Miss Clementina Black and many others helped in the heavy work.

(Besant, p. 336)

Within a fortnight the London Trades Council was called in as arbitrator and the firm virtually capitulated. Fines and deductions were abolished, wages raised, but most important in the short term was the formation of the Matchmakers' Union (one of the most difficult sections of workers to organise), the largest in England of its kind, composed entirely of women. The long-term effects were incalculable. At the least it set off a pattern of unionisation by the unskilled whose effects extended well beyond the boundaries of East London.

The lesson was not lost elsewhere in London, as the struggle for union building gathered pace and entered the political arena. Besant sustained her momentum:

Then came a cry for help from South London, from tin-box makers, illegally fined, and in many cases grievously mutilated by the non-fencing of machinery; then aid to shop assistants, also illegally fined . . . a vigorous agitation for a free meal for children, and for fair wages to be paid by all public bodies; work for the dockers and exposure of their wrongs, a visit to the Cradley Heath chain makers, speeches to them, writing for them; a contest for the School Board for the Tower Hamlets division and triumphant return at the head of the poll. Such were the ways in which the autumn days were spent . . . lectures . . . meetings . . . and scores of articles written for the winning of daily bread.

(Besant, p. 338)

Momentous happenings—not least for women. Following her example their incursion into East London was dramatic. Eleanor Marx-Aveling joined the foragers. Unlike her father, Karl Marx, who appears never to have crossed the border into plebeian London, she chose to explore there, sometimes alone, occasionally with novelist Margaret Harkness. Hitherto that shadowy global image of the oppressed poor had been conveyed to her by dry statistics and theoretical texts. Here she saw the reality for the first time: in terms of individual human beings, suffering terribly in the everyday fight for survival. In the East End Marx's daughter first crossed 'the line between serving a cause and identifying herself with the women and men that cause was intended to serve . . . Eleanor had never known real hunger: debts and duns and short commons, yes, and sometimes "doing without", but not the ravening need of those clinging to the brink of survival who asked bread and were given a stone.' Eleanor, unlike her father, openly declared her ethnic relationship with the Jews, and was sensible enough to learn Yiddish in order to help in the effort to unionise the immigrant tailors (*Kapp, vol. II, pp. 261–2*).

After serving an activist apprenticeship in Whitechapel it was her practical voluntarism during the making of the London Gasworkers' Union that revealed her remarkable qualities as teacher, platform orator and organiser. In three months (March – June 1889) the Herculean task of unionising the unskilled gas workers was successfully effected as 90% of the total labour force joined as paid members. By July brilliant organisation and a mere strike threat won the gas workers all their demands without the need to strike: an 8-hour day and an extra shilling on the hour. Their leader, Will Thorne, surmised that 'she (Eleanor) would have been a greater woman's leader than the greatest of the contemporary women'. (In Will Thorne's *My Life's Battles* he makes moving reference to the friendship and help he derived from Eleanor.) She became his friend and confidante, assisted in his formal education, created a women's section of the Union, acted as the first Secretary, and was later elected President of the Union—no mean achievement in a male-dominated society!

It could be argued that, where the women led, the men followed. After the triumphs of the match girls and gas workers came the legendary Dock Strike. Conditions in the London docks epitomised the working out of laissez-faire principles and 'healthy competition' between labour. (A 'healthy' (?) free market concept eulogised by contemporary Victorian economists, and more recently resuscitated, with updated qualifications, by the Chicago school led by their pundit Milton Friedman.) By 1889 dockers were already threatened by a shrinking industry, in which labour supply outstripped demand, the latter dependent on the number of ship arrivals and depar-

Dock Strike, 1889

tures. Improvements in shipbuilding, with iron and then steel replacing wood in basic structures, led to the migration of builders from the Thames side to the North East coast. Growing mechanisation at the docks and surrounding factories ensured a steady supply of surplus labour seeking employment: to be utilised by the sweaters (sub-contractors) as *dock-rats*, i.e. to undercut regular casuals and thereby depress wages. 'Every class, even artisans and clerks . . . compete at the dock gates', observed Charles Booth, so that brutalised men fighting for work was an everyday scene on the docks of East London—the richest port in the world.

Awaiting the 'call-on' for a day's work brought an army of desperate men to the water-side, scrounging in the dustbins for food, or furtively grubbing in refuse for droppings of grain or tobacco outside the wharves. As the 'caller-on' walked up to select the daily work

gang, men flung themselves at the bar of the cage (an iron-railed shed which protected the sweater), struggling to get to the front so as to catch the eye of their tormentor, who strutted up and down casually noting and selecting the most ravenous (i.e. potentially cheapest) candidates for the labour 'ticket'. Ben Tillett, who had personally suffered the obscenities of the cage recalls:

> Coats, flesh and even ears were torn off. The strong literally threw themselves over the heads of their fellows and battled . . . through the kicking, punching, cursing crowds to the rails of the 'cage' which held them like rats—mad human rats who saw food in the ticket . . .
>
> *(Tillett (1), p. 12)*

All this, for what? For one or, at the most, two hours' work at 5d. an hour; and at the end of the day, Tillett shared memories of weak, exhausted men collapsing at

118

the paybox, or others dying at their own door step, still clutching their few miserable pieces of blood money.

Degradation begat degradation. Tillett recalls (*Tillett (2), p. 173*) how certain contractors retained hired thugs who 'hounded and whipped the men . . . Young men were put to run old and weaker men down, either carrying loads or running trucks. Dreadful furies were let loose on the docks. I have often heard the . . . curse . . . "Kill the old sod!"' In July 1887, Tillett, sensing a climate of support, appealed to Liberal MPs and other public figures to act as patrons in the creation of a Tea Coopers and General Labourers' Association. Aided by a few stalwarts he went forth as a crusader into the hostile docks. From the beginning it was a struggle for survival against brute force and ignorance: 'It was almost impossible to obtain a hearing . . . Insult, physical violence, and filthy refuse, stones . . . were thrown at us. Contractors . . . hired their boozed bullies to break up our meetings.' But supportive action in high places sustained him. Annie Besant and Charles Bradlaugh joined him on public platforms. W.

C. Steadman (Secretary of the Barge-Builders) and Ben Cooper (Cigar Makers) accompanied him around dockland and offered practical advice on the possibilities of union building there. Prominent Liberals contributed funds, particularly local MP Samuel Montagu who gave a first instalment of £5. Above all he won the friendship of Cardinal Manning, Archbishop of Westminster, who espoused the cause of Trade Unionism as much to divert it from the dangers of a political alliance between the 'outcast population and (atheistic) Socialism' as to promote better conditions for working folk.

The Dock Strike (the only one until the 1926 General Strike which was accorded 'the dignity of capital letters'—Tillett) was sparked off on 12 August 1889, by a dispute aboard the sailing ship Lady Armstrong berthed in the South West India Docks. It arose from the 'plus' system, whereby most of the $\frac{1}{2}$d. piece rate earned by labourers engaged in speedier jobs was pocketed by the 'sweaters'. The dockers, whose regular pay was 5d. and hour and 6d. for overtime worked after 8 p.m., walked off the ship. They demanded a normal 6d. an hour, 8d. for overtime, with no 'call' to be less than four hours a day, and, above all, an end to the inhuman contract system. On 14 August, under Ben Tillett's leadership, the strike was declared official. The Docker's Tanner became a rallying cry as the strike spread rapidly and an army of dockers mobilised for the fray.

On 16 August, John Burns, leader of the Amalgamated Society of Engineers, who had initially rejected an appeal to support the strike, after consulting with Tillett at strike headquarters (the *Wades Arms* pub in Poplar) found himself heading a procession of 6,000 marchers as he walked back to confront the dock directors in the City along the since famous East End route: West India Dock Road, Commercial Road, Fenchurch Street, and Leadenhall Street. Subsequent marches attracted armies of over 100,000. Mammoth meetings addressed by Ben Tillett and union leaders John Burns, Tom Mann and Will Thorne, national and international financial support of which eloquent testimony is recorded in the strike committee's Statement of Account, totalling £48,736. 3s. 1d. (of which £30,000 was contributed by the Australian 'wharfies'), and the efforts of a sympathetic and persuasive mediator, Cardinal Manning, brought ultimate victory to the dockers. On 16 September the five week drama ended with all their demands met.

It could be argued that in adding to the victory of the match girls the dockers ushered in a new age in industrial relations. The radical *Reynolds Newspaper* registered the message (*1 September 1889*):

> Messrs Burns, Mann and Tillett and their many hard-working colleagues have, by their splendid action, vindicated the dignity of labour, and, it may be, created a new industrial era. For this they are entitled to the gratitude of the country and to a niche in the temple of history . . . *They have given the millions of unskilled labourers a place of honour among the industries of the country that trade unionism in the older sense has always denied them . . .*

Rank-and-file East End labourers were the pioneers of the New Unionism. Their involvement in the new radicalism, i.e. in the growth of Socialism, is less easily discernible. The daily struggle for bread left them little time or inclination for the luxury of political diversions. Yet as one of the classical urban deprived areas it should, during the course of the nineteenth century, at least have developed the ground swell of a social movement. There are some signs of this from the 1880s onwards in the reports of the radical journals (e.g. in *Justice, Freedom, Commonweal* and the Yiddish *Arbeter Fraint*) and in the local press; but more potent is the evidence in the novels of social realism such as those of Margaret Harkness. She appears to illustrate that by the 1880s there was an unquantifiable number of politically educated working men and women who constituted regular consumers of radical publications and were active participants in their organisations, notably the Social Democratic Federation and the Socialist League.

In Darkest London portrays some radical images with emphasis on local militant feminists. Harkness is rather patronising towards her working-class sisters, coming down rather hard on their simplistic assumptions and humourless dedication. On the other hand there are deft sketches of élite characters among the various Socialist groups—SDF, Socialist League, Anarchist and Fabian—with scathing criticism of their personal jealousies and vanities which sustained an inbred factionalism that brought only weakness and confusion to the movement.

Like the 'saints', and sometimes in alliance with them, the socialist intellectuals came to bring the 'message' to the East End barbarian. Group members set up their platforms in Victoria Park (Sundays) and on street

Parliament Court, off Artillery Passage, today, where the Ethical Society first met in 1793

Offices of the anarchist newspaper, Angel Alley

corner sites allotted them by custom, and also held evening educational sessions in their club rooms on week days. In the great Socialist divide of 1888 we read that Socialist Leaguers hold a weekly Sunday meeting outside the *Salmon and Ball* in the morning; while after 24 November, the SDF advertises a future weekly Sunday meeting there in the evening. Both parties call meetings consecutively at the popular open-air site on the Mile End Waste; and while Dod Street, Poplar, saw large weekly gatherings sponsored by the SDF, those at Leman Street and Shadwell were given over exclusively to the Socialist League. One of the great visiting propagandists in East London was William Morris, who often spoke in the Mile End Radical Club, 108 Bridge Street, at mass meetings of commemoration or protest on the Waste, and, always with delight, to an (uncomprehending!) audience of Yiddish-speaking Socialists and Anarchists at the Berner Street Club off the Commercial Road. By 1914 the area was well served with a mélange of radical pundits and preachers. While Bernard Shaw pricked the Establishment with his verbal shafts from Toynbee Hall and George Lansbury laboured strenuously at his Christian Socialist vineyard beyond Bow; while Ben Tillett fought desperately to consolidate his fickle dock labourers into a mighty Union and Eleanor Marx-Aveling was teaching, cajoling, organising her beloved gas men, one group of workers were developing a highly sophisticated movement of their own. They were a caucus of Russo-Jewish immigrants.

It was under the editorship of folk poet Morris Winchevsky (later also co-founder in 1897 of *Forwards*—the famous Yiddish journal in New York, which is still published) that the first Yiddish Socialist journal ever, the *Poilishe Yidl* (the little Polish Jew), appeared in the streets of Spitalfields on 25 July 1884, the press appropriately sited at 137 Commercial Street—the hub of Jewish settlement. Its main objectives were to instruct the 'greener' in the political and social obligations required of him in the new land and to warn him of the pitfalls to avoid in a hostile environment. There was no going back after this pioneer inception. It sustained itself for fourteen issues and folded up, to be almost immediately replaced by its political substitute the *Arbeter Fraint*, first published on 15 July 1885, and destined to last for forty-seven years. Both papers initiated a tabloid for Jewish self-observation and criticism, as well as providing a sounding board for the few working-class intellectuals

William Morris (1834–1896)

dedicated to bringing social and political consciousness to their own folk.

Their efforts exceeded those of their gentile comrades and flourished in the harsh milieu. A handful of earnest young men and women created activist Socialist and Anarchist groups in Whitechapel. During autumn 1889, they led the first historical strike of immigrant tailors to victory. By the turn of the century the Anarchists supplied the major leadership in the strike movements and in the struggle to unionise the Jewish tailors, bakers, and cabinet makers. Equally important was the functioning of the Anarchist Club in Jubilee Street between 1906 and 1914 with its international implications. It provided a rendezvous and haven for continental revolutionists on the run. The ascendancy of the extraordinary Rudolf Rocker, gentile Anarchist yet charismatic leader of the Jewish radicals, helped prefix East London on the preparatory end to New York's finishing school for socialist and libertarian education; and a Trade Union élite who served their political apprenticeship in the London

Rudolf Rocker and *chaverim*, c. 1912

ghetto went on to greater triumphs in the New World. On closer scrutiny Whitechapel discloses a galaxy of historic figures who often visited or made temporary base there. Among them we detect Kropotkin, Malatesta and Louise Michel who maintained close contact with the Yiddish Anarchists; and it was Rocker's voluntaristic commitment to their cause that first promulgated, and then brought to a victorious conclusion, the second great strike action of the Jewish tailors in 1912.

A phantasmagoria of the world's greats accompanies you beneath the few remaining shadowy archways and cobbled alleys of old Stepney. In the imagination they conjure up the living machinations of some of the architects of great events. The hall of what is now a furniture warehouse in Fulbourne Street, opposite the London Hospital in Whitechapel, once echoed to the alien voices of Russian and Polish delegates gathered together for the making of the 5th Congress of the Russian Social Democratic Labour Party, which consolidated the triumph of the Bolshevik party. Thus

it was, with local Socialist George Lansbury acting as intermediary, that wealthy Philadelphian naphtha manufacturer George Fels (also follower of US radical 'single taxer' Henry George) met and was strongly impressed by Lenin. (Lenin had previously spent a whole year in London (1902–1903). He was known to have addressed two meetings in Whitechapel, an area he enjoyed visiting, the second on 21 March 1903, at the Alexander Hall, Jubilee Street. This building was later transformed into the Anarchist Club and Lenin was again seen there in 1907 and 1908 according to surviving members interviewed by me. W.J.F.) The result was an immediate loan of £1,700 sterling, to sustain the party's funds. One condition was that all the delegates sign the bond acknowledging the debt. A copy of the document found later among Fels's papers in Philadelphia reveals the signatories as the founding fathers of the Soviet Union, including Stalin and Trotsky together—a rare phenomenon! Although the loan could not be repaid within the specified time limit, the debt was honoured to the full fifteen years later by order of the dying Lenin himself. Across from the first Salvation Army hostel, built to accommodate homeless vagrants, is the Tower House—another public doss house—in Fieldgate Street, which for fourteen days during that same Congress housed two other Russian pseudo-tramps named Joseph Djugashvili and Maxim Litvinov, who shared adjoining cubicles beneath its gloomy, unsalubrious walls. It still provides lodgings for the transient, although the nightly cost of a room has increased tenfold since they slept there.

At Bow and Poplar, the eastern limits of Tower Hamlets, the pubs and houses still remain where the other great pioneer of women's liberation, Sylvia Pankhurst, mobilised her working-class women for an onslaught on male chauvinism and for women's suffrage. Midway along the borough lies Sidney Street, which set the scene for the second great drama in East London mythology (see above pp. 107–8). As indicated above, extreme radicalism in response to political and social deprivation often manifests itself by acts which, by any definition, are criminally inhuman, and politically counter-productive.

The inter-war years registered dramatic happenings in the radical politics of East London. First was the occasion of the triumph of the Labour Party, which, since 1918, has continually held majority power in both local government, and, with one exception (Sir Percy Harris—persistently elected Liberal MP for

Surviving corner of Fulbourne Street, where the Fifth
Congress of the R.S.D.L.P. was mobilised in May 1907.
The founding fathers of the Soviet Union were all present

S.W. Bethnal Green), in the parliamentary constituencies. Second was the impact of the General Strike which during its nine days (3–12 May 1926) created its own legends out of the confrontations and bloody clashes with the police and military. The London Docks being a main entrepôt for food, it was anticipated (rightly) that massed units of the British Army, infantry and armoured, would move in to clear foodstuffs piled up on Thames side against an opposing army of strikers rendered impotent to stop them by the invaders' backing of 'enough artillery to kill every other living being in the neighbourhood' (*New York World*). Grim memories die hard. Survivors never forgot this brutal *tour de force*, nor forgave its most bellicose advocate—the then Chancellor of the Exchequer, Winston Churchill, who, in the columns of the anti-strike journal *British Gazette*, declared that *any* action taken by the armed forces 'will receive, both now and afterwards, the full support of His Majesty's Government'.

Thirdly, there was the climactic episode, destined to transcend the locale and impose itself on historical legend: the battle of Cable Street. Economic depression and high unemployment provided fertile soil for the growth of extreme radical ideologies—Right and Left. The East End was a suitable testing ground for both. Against a background of permanent deprivation, the Jews provided a ready-made scapegoat for Mosley's Fascists who, in turn, furnished the Communists with their *bête noire* (i.e. 'agents of decaying Capitalism',

Troops in the East India Dock Road, General Strike, 1926

Outside the East India Dock gates, General Strike, 1926

The battle of Cable Street, 4 October 1936

etc.). Subsequent attempts to explain away local Fascist aberration in terms of individual psychological misfits or the activities of a mindless *lumpenproletariat* no longer ring true. Perhaps the *Jewish Chronicle*, though no friend of the Fascists, managed to convey a more balanced appraisal of the basis of their support:

> There has been a combination of several types of working class element influenced by Fascism. They included some unemployed and many wives of unemployed workers, many *lumpenproletariat*, a number of municipal workers who held a Trade Union card and were dissatisfied with conditions under a Labour Borough Council, some Catholics, many unorganised workers in small workshops and factories . . . costermongers and smallholders who felt that the Jews were depriving them of their livelihood and a large number of shopkeepers . . . voted Fascist.
>
> (*16 April 1937*)

Yet only a minority of these were real activists who swallowed the Fascist theology and accompanied Mosley on his *grandes journées*.

In late September 1936, the homespun Führer announced his plan to lead a great march of his Fascist Army through the East End on Sunday 4 October. It was an act of provocation, and East Enders of all creeds responded accordingly. On that bright autumn morning 3,000 Blackshirts mobilised on their start line in Royal Mint Street poised to march out in four columns by way of Cable Street. Their flanks were to be protected en route by nearly 7,000 policemen recruited into the area and including the entire Metropolitan corps of mounted police. Radio vans patrolled and an autogyro flew overhead to monitor the opposing forces. At the confluence of Cable and Leman Street barricades were being erected and a huge crowd collected at Gardiners Corner—the real point of entry into East London. By mid-afternoon it was estimated that a hostile army of at least 100,000 had gathered along the proposed route. Anti-fascist placards hung from windows and walls; and the current slogan of the Spanish Republic 'THEY SHALL NOT PASS!' was proclaimed everywhere on a sea of banners. The 'battle of Cable Street' broke out when a lorry dragged from a yard was overturned in the middle of the road, forming the base of a barricade. Police charges were met by a hail of stones and bricks from defenders on the ground and from the upper storeys of surrounding houses. It was the dockers of Wapping and St. George's who constituted the vanguard of opposition here, thus preventing the march from taking off. After some police skirmishing and subsequent injuries and arrests, Sir Phillip Game, Commissioner of Police, was convinced that it would be impossible for Mosley to proceed without mass riots and bloodshed. He ordered Mosley to turn about and the procession marched off to the music of pipes and drums, in the opposite direction, along the Embankment, where, in the absence of an audience, they quickly dispersed. That night there was dancing in the side streets as East Enders celebrated their victory and the birth of a 'heroic' legend. Recent writers have dismissed many stories emanating from the legend as figments of the imagination. That may be so. What *is* true (I was at Gardiners Corner on that day) is that it was the spontaneous turnout of the East End as a whole, and not only the Jews, that stopped the Fascist march.

During the thirties the Communist Party gathered strength in membership and alliances, mainly in response to the Blackshirt menace which acted as a catalyst in binding together diverse anti-Fascist elements: such as Jews organising to combat anti-Semitism; Labour, ILP and Communist supporters of the Popular Front alarmed at the Fascist successes in Europe; and charismatic figures like Father St. John Groser and the Warden of Toynbee Hall. Consequently, in 1937, Stepney elected its first Communist borough councillor, Phil Piratin, who went on to even greater triumph in July 1945, when he was returned as first (and last?) Communist MP for Mile End. His elevation was as much a reflection of local satisfaction with the practical work carried out by Communists at root level, especially in their successful leadership during the rent strikes of 1938–9 in which they

organised tenants' groups effectively to prevent unfair rent rises and evictions, as an attempt to put an end to the self-perpetuating Labour Establishment of pre-war days.

But after the 1950s the *status quo* was retrieved and Labour more firmly entrenched. Tower Hamlets, as though bound by ecclesiastical ritual, appears destined to follow a changeless course. On closer examination its radical inheritance accrues from more than that. For centuries of deprivation, neglect, the struggle for bread and the heartlessness of a once laissez-faire society have educated its victims. It is now parochially ingrained, as holy writ, that, whatever its shortcomings, it was Labour who helped succour the East End poor in an uncaring society. There is evidence to sustain this and it would appear to confirm the slogan 'No Tories for Tower Hamlets' as a reality—permanently ordained.

Offices of the Jewish Secular Radicals, 22 Alie Street, 1937/8

Radical graffiti from Jubilee Year

BIBLIOGRAPHY

BANTON, M. P. *The Coloured Quarter* (London 1953).

BARNETT, H. O. *Canon Barnett: His Life, Works and Friends* (2 vols) (London 1918).

BERMANT, Chaim *Point of Arrival* (London 1975).

BESANT, A. *Annie Besant*, an autobiography (London 1893).

BINDER, Pearl *The Pearlies* (London 1975).

BOOTH, Charles (1) 'Condition and Occupation of the Peoples of Tower Hamlets' *Journal of the Royal Statistical Society* L2, 1887.

(2) *Life and Labour of the People of London* (London 1892–7).

(3) 'The inhabitants of Tower Hamlets (School Board Division): their condition and occupations' *Journal of the Royal Statistical Society* June 1887.

BOOTH, William *In Darkest England* (London 1890).

COATES, T. F. G. *The Prophet of the Poor* (London 1905).

HARKNESS, Margaret, see John Law.

HITCHMAN, Janet *They Carried the Sword* (London 1966).

HUDDLESTON, T. *Naught for your Comfort* (London 1956).

KAPP, Yvonne *Eleanor Marx* (London 1976).

KRAY, Charles *Me and My Brothers* (London 1976).

LAW, John (1) *In Darkest London* (London 1889).

(2) *Out of Work* (London 1888).

LONDON, Jack *The People of the Abyss* (London 1903).

MACKAY, J. H. *The Anarchists* (Boston 1891).

MORRISON, A. (1) 'A street' *Macmillan's Magazine* October 1891, later reprinted as introduction to Morrison, *Tales of Mean Streets* (London 1894).

(2) 'Lizerunt' *National Observer* 22 July 1893.

PRESTON, William C. *The Bitter Cry of Outcast London* (London 1883).

REANEY, G. S. in Arnold White *The Destitute Alien in Great Britain* (London 1892).

THORNE, Guy *The Great Acceptance* (London 1912).

THORNE, W. *My Life's Battles* (London 1926).

TILLETT, B. (1) *A Brief History of the Dockers' Union* (Dock, Wharf, Riverside and General Workers' Union 1910).

(2) *Memoirs and Reflections* (London 1931).

WEBB, B. and S. *Problems of Modern Industry* (London 1902).

WENSLEY, F. B. *Detective Days* (London 1931).

WILLIAMS, A. E. *Barnardo of Stepney* (London 1945).

WILLIAMSON, J. *Father Joe* (London 1961).

ZANGWILL, I. *Children of the Ghetto* (London 1892).

Chapter 2: Poverty

J. H. Mackay, *The Anarchists* (Benjamin R. Tucker 1891).

H. O. Barnett, *Canon Barnett: his life, works and friends* (John Murray 1918).

Jack London, *The People of the Abyss* (Macmillan 1903)

John Law, (1) *In Darkest London* (William Reeves 1889).

(2) *Out of Work* (Swan Sonnenschein & Co. 1888).

William C. Preston, *The Bitter Cry of Outcast London* (James Clarke & Co. Ltd. 1883).

William Booth, *In Darkest England* (International Headquarters of the Salvation Army 1890).

Pearl Binder, *The Pearlies* (Jupiter Press 1975).

A. Morrison, (1) 'A street' *Macmillan's Magazine* October 1891.

(2) 'Lizerunt' *National Observer* 22 July 1893.

Charles Booth, (1) 'Condition and Occupation of the Peoples of Tower Hamlets' *Journal of the Royal Statistical Society* L2, 1887.

(2) *Life and Labour of the People of London* (Macmillan 1892–7).

Chapter 3: Philanthropy

A. E. Williams, *Barnardo of Stepney* (Allen and Unwin 1943).

Jessie Powell, *The Man Who Didn't Go to China* (Lutterworth 1947).

Janet Hitchman, *They Carried the Sword* (Gollancz 1966).

Thomas Barnardo, *Three Tracts* (Dr Barnardo's 1888).

H. O. Barnett, *Canon Barnett: his life, works and friends* (John Murray 1918).

William Booth, *In Darkest England* (International Headquarters of the Salvation Army 1890).

Thomas F. G. Coates, *The Prophet of the Poor* (Hodder and Stoughton 1905).

John Law (pseudonym of Margaret Harkness), *In Darkest London* (William Reeves 1889).

E. Bishop, *Blood and Fire* (Longmans 1964).

Oasis in the Desert, report published by the *Christian Herald* 1886.

G. Thorne, *The Great Acceptance: the life story of F. N. Charrington* (Hodder and Stoughton 1912).

F. G. Bettany, *Stewart Headlam: a biography* (John Murray 1926).

P. Jones, *The Christian Socialist Revival, 1877–1914* (Princeton 1968).

K. Brill, *John Groser, East London Priest* (Mowbrays 1971).

Fr. St. John Groser, *Politics and Person* (SCM Press 1944).

Trevor Huddleston, *Naught for your Comfort* (Collins 1956).

Chapter 4: **Immigrants**

Israel Zangwill, *Children of the Ghetto* (Heinemann 1892).

Lloyd P. Gartner, *The Jewish Immigrant in England 1870–1914* (Allen and Unwin 1960).

William J. Fishman, *East End Jewish Radicals* (Duckworth 1975).

John A Garrard, *The English and Immigration* (O.U.P. 1971).

Bernard Gainer, *The Alien Invasion* (Heinemann 1972).

Colin Holmes (ed.), *Immigrants and Minorities in British Society* (Allen and Unwin 1978).

Chaim Bermant, *Point of Arrival* (Eyre Methuen 1975).

Chapter 5: **Crime**

William Steward, *Jack the Ripper: a new theory* (Quality Press 1939).

Donald McCormick, *The Identity of Jack the Ripper* (John Lang 1959).

Robin Odell, *Jack the Ripper: in fact and fiction* (Harrap 1965).

Dan Farson, *Jack the Ripper* (Michael Joseph 1972).

Donald Rumbelow, *The Complete Jack the Ripper* (W. H. Allen 1975).

Stephen Knight, *Jack the Ripper: the final solution* (Harrap 1976).

J. P. Eddy, *The Mystery of Peter the Painter* (Stevens 1946).

Donald Rumbelow, *The Houndsditch Murders and the Siege of Sidney Street* (Macmillan 1973).

Sir William Nott-Bower, *Fifty-two Years a Policeman* (Edward Arnold 1926).

J. E. Holroyd, *The Gaslight Murders* (Allen and Unwin 1960).

Eric Linklater, *The Corpse on Clapham Common* (Macmillan 1971).

John Pearson, *The Profession of Violence* (Weidenfeld and Nicolson 1972).

Brian McConnell, *The Rise and Fall of the Brothers Kray* (David Bruce and Watson 1969).

Leslie Payne, *The Brotherhood* (Michael Joseph 1973).

Charles Kray, *Me and My Brothers* (Everest Books 1976).

Chapter 6: **Radicals**

Annie Besant, an autobiography (T. Fisher-Unwin 1893).

Yvonne Kapp, *Eleanor Marx*, vol. 2 (Lawrence and Wishart 1976).

B. Tillett, *A Brief History of the Dockers' Union* (Dock, Wharf, Riverside and General Workers' Union, Sept. 1910).

William J. Fishman, *East End Jewish Radicals* (Duckworth 1975).

Andrew Rothstein, *Lenin in Britain*, pamphlet (Central Books, 37 Gray's Inn Road, n.d.).

William J. Fishman, 'Lenin in London', *Anglia* 24, no. 4 (October 1967).

R. Benewick, *The Fascist Movement in Britain* (Allen Lane 1972).

Colin Holmes (ed.), *Immigrants and Minorities in British Society* (Allen and Unwin 1978).

Walking Tour 1

Rendezvous: Whitechapel Art Gallery

1 Angel Alley, once inhabited by Irish and later Jewish immigrants. Henrietta Barnett, in the 1870s, was very worried about its disorderly inhabitants, who often kept the rent collectors and the police at bay for months. Now houses the libertarian *Freedom* press.

2 Here at the rear of *Bloom's* was located George Yard Buildings, where, in the early hours of 6 August 1888, was found the corpse of prostitute Martha Turner, peppered with 29 knife wounds—considered the first victim of Jack the Ripper.

3 Toynbee Hall. Founded in 1884 by Canon Barnett as a residence for Oxbridge graduates, who volunteered to do social and educational work in the East End. Here, too, were mobilised researchers for Charles Booth's still classic study: *Life and Labour of the People of London* (completed 1889).

4 Skeleton of Lolesworth Buildings, completed between 1886 and 1887, as *model dwellings* by the East End Dwellings Company, formed by a group of parish workers at the Rev. Barnett's St. Jude's Church 'to provide a building of brick or stone to house at least 380 mechanics, labourers and other persons of the working class in designs already approved by the Board of Works'.

5 Thrawl and Flower and Dean Streets. Once the most disreputable streets in nineteenth century legend. Consisted of cheap lodging houses, brothels and thieves' dens. Visited by American writer, Jack London, in his disguised role as a tramp for his social recording in 1902 of *The People of the Abyss*, and by Lenin during the same year.

In the buildings of Flower and Dean Street (Fashion Court), Abe Sapperstein, later founder of the *Harlem Globetrotters*, world famous black basket-ball team, was born in 1908.

6 Fashion Street. Described by the chronicler of the Jewish ghetto, Israel Zangwill, in the opening lines of his classic *Children of the Ghetto* (1892). The three-storied houses on the north side still remain, with the traditional clothing workshops perpetuated by the new immigrants from Pakistan and Bangla-Desh.

The eminent post-war playwright, Arnold Wesker, spent his formative years here.

On the south side—the Byzantine-like façade housed what was originally intended by builder Abraham Davis (1905) to be a covered arcade with cross passages to provide 250 small lock-up shops, a reading room and bathroom to attract trade from the Lane. But Davis went broke, and the arcade was reconstructed as a factory (once housing Scammel & Nephew Ltd.).

7 At the corner of Fournier Street and Brick Lane is the scheduled 'ancient monument', originally a Huguenot chapel built in 1742. It became a Methodist chapel in 1809 and 1897 it was bought by the Jewish ultra-Orthodox immigrant *Machzikei Hadath* society and named the Spitalfields Great Synagogue. The religious function of the building has been maintained by its current use as a mosque.

8 Wilkes Street still preserves many of the old Huguenot houses built in the 1720s. Here John Wilkes once spoke to mass audiences of his supporters during his campaign for civil liberty.

9 3 Princelet Street once housed the first Yiddish theatre, where one of its great actors, Jacob Adler, played to full immigrant audiences between 1886 and 1887. On 18 January 1887, a false cry of fire during an evening performance led to a stampede towards the entrance and within a few minutes 17 people were crushed to death. In March 1887 Adler and his troupe left

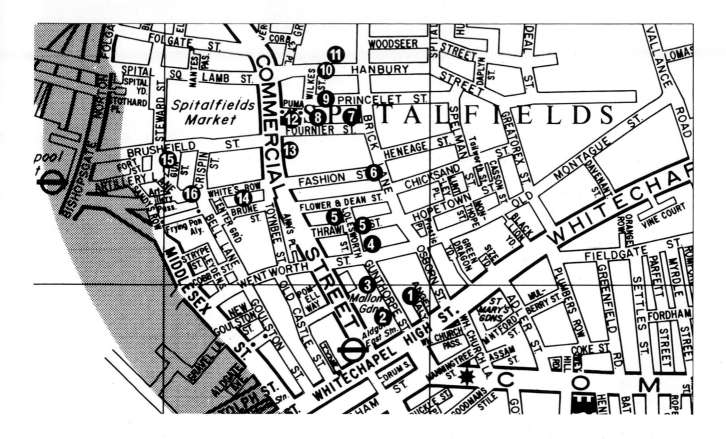

for New York to help found the great Yiddish theatre tradition there, with its subsequent influence on the American theatre and the Hollywood film industry.

10   Christ Church Hall, Hanbury Street, which was hired out for the great radical and strike meetings of the 1880s and 1890s. Speakers included Lewis Lyons, Jewish tailors' leader, Annie Besant, during the match girls' strike, and Eleanor Marx-Aveling.

11   At the rear of the lodging house at 29 Hanbury Street was found the body of 'Dark' Annie Chapman, third victim of the Ripper murders.

12   The *Jack the Ripper* pub. The window on the Commercial Street side is engraved with the chronicle of the Ripper murders, and the internal decor is in accord with that prevalent in 1888. It was here that Mary Kelly, the final victim, was last seen alive.

13   Christ Church, Spitalfields, built by Nicholas Hawksmoor, contemporary of Christopher Wren, and completed about 1729. Attached to

the church is the now much reduced Christ Church gardens, popularly known in legend as 'Itchy Park' a traditional sleeping place for the poor and destitute homeless of London.

14   The Jewish soup kitchen of Brune Street opened in 1902 to feed the Jewish poor in the area. It now opens one day a week (Tuesday) and is still maintained by charitable aid.

15   At 40 Gun Street, Spitalfields, a small one-storied slum house, demolished in 1976, the meeting of the Hebrew Socialist Union—the first separatist Jewish group—took place on 20 May 1876, under the leadership of Aron Lieberman, considered the prophet of Socialist Zionism.

16   Artillery Lane and Street where Henry VIII's Royal Artillery Company used to hold gunnery practice. Opposite the barrack-like Women's Night Refuge (where a dedicated staff still offers food and shelter to the homeless of both sexes), in contrast, stands 56 Artillery Street, built in 1756 and considered to have 'the finest Georgian shop-front in London'.

Walking Tour 2

WHITECHAPEL AND MILE END

Rendezvous: Whitechapel Station

1   Adjoining the Station (right) was once the Working Lads' Institute built in 1885 for recreational and educational facilities. In 1888 an extension was opened to include a swimming bath and lecture hall. In the latter great radical meetings were held in the 1890s and speakers included Prince Kropotkin and Rudolf Rocker.

2   Bucks Row (now Durward Street). Outside the school great Sunday meetings, both political and Trade Union, were held before 1914.

3   Near the confluence of Bucks Row and West Durward Street the mutilated body of Jack the Ripper's second victim—Mary Ann Nichols—was found in the early hours of 31 August 1888.

4   Fulbourne Street. Here at a Jewish Socialist Club the Congress of the Russian Social Democratic Labour Party mobilised as a reporting centre in May 1907. Delegates included Lenin, Stalin, Trotsky, Litvinoff and Gorky.

5   London Hospital. Founded in 1752; by 1757 the new Hospital was inaugurated with 161 beds. The Medical College was begun in 1784—the first medical school formed on the model of a University faculty. Dr Barnardo, founder of the children's homes, was a student here and it is now internationally famous as a teaching hospital.

6   Vicarage of St. Augustine and St. Philip, where a plaque on the wall informs us that the famous Oxford Historian of the English People, J. R. Green, lived here from 1866–9.

7   Once location of 100 Sidney Street, a red-brick four-storeyed house, where the famous Sidney Street Siege took place. Two Lettish Social Democrats, Fritz Svaas and Joseph Marx, who had been involved in an attempted robbery of a jeweller's shop and the murder of three policemen in Houndsditch the month before, were cornered here on 3 January 1911. They barricaded themselves in on the first floor and fought off the combined efforts of armed police and 20 Scots Guards to dislodge them for six hours. The house eventually caught fire and two charred bodies were discovered in the ruins. The leader of the gang who had masterminded the original Houndsditch affair, believed until recently to be Peter Piatkov, disappeared, thereby giving rise to the famous legend of that East End anti-hero, Peter the Painter.

8   Site of the New Alexandra Hall, Jubilee Street, once a Salvation Army Hostel, where on 7 March 1903 Lenin was main speaker at the meeting celebrating the 32nd anniversary of the Paris Commune; and where later, in 1907, he was seen as a visitor at the newly founded Anarchist Club formed under the auspices of Rudolf Rocker, the German Libertarian philosopher, teacher and Trade Union leader of the immigrant Jews of the East End from 1895 to 1914.

9   Dunstan Houses, where a quasi-Libertarian Commune was centred at the turn of the century. Rocker lived at flat No. 33 until he was arrested in 1914. In the flat below, Kropotkin's journal, *Lestki Chliebi Volya*, was printed and he was a regular visitor there.

10   Between 4 and 17 May 1299, Edward I held a second parliament at the house of Henry le Waleis, Mayor of London, in Stepney Green, where he confirmed the granting of the Great Charter and a Charter of the Forests.

   Stepney Green also sets the scene for the plays of ex-East Enders and famous post-war playwrights, Bernard Kops ('The Hamlet of Stepney Green') and Arnold Weskers' first play of his trilogy ('Chicken Soup and Barley').

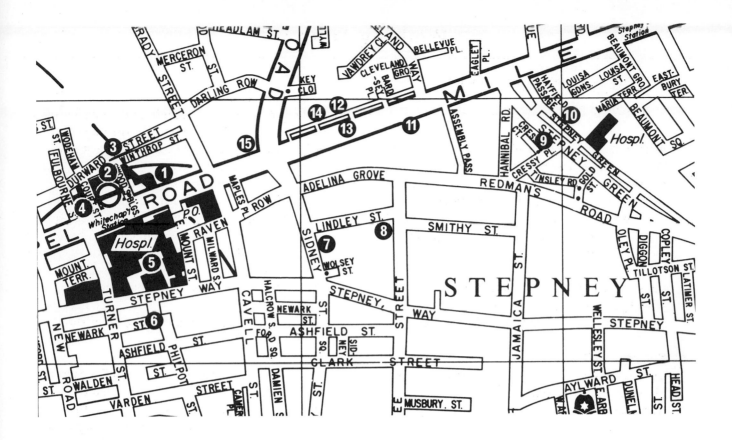

11 Captain James Cook lived at 88 Mile End Road in between his famous voyages. A black plaque on the remaining outside wall commemorates his residence here.

12 The New Assembly Hall (Tower Hamlets Mission) replaced the Great Assembly Hall founded by the Temperance campaigner Frederick Charrington (of the brewery family!) in 1883, and irreparably damaged in the Second World War.

Here great social and political meetings took place. On 1 November 1890, William Morris, Eleanor Marx-Aveling (daughter of Karl Marx), John Burns and Prince Kropotkin, spoke on a common platform outside at a meeting called to protest against the Russian persecution of the Jews.

13 In a waste enclosure opposite the Assembly Hall, where William Booth set up his first platform, is embedded a stone inscribed: 'Here William Booth commenced the work of the Salvation Army, July 1865.'

14 The Almshouses of the Trinity Brethren, built in 1695 by Christopher Wren on grounds presented by Elder Brother, Captain Mudd of Ratcliff, intended for 'twenty eight decayed masters and commanders of ships, or the widows of such. Now maisonettes leased out by the G.L.C.

15 The *Blind Beggar*, the old pub, witnessed the first incursion of Salvation Army lassies selling *War Cry*. It was the shooting of George Cornell by Ronald Kray in the saloon bar here on the evening of 6 March 1966, that finally led to the exposure and conviction of the Kray brothers.

PHOTO ACKNOWLEDGMENTS

p. 31, Bedford Institute Association; pp. 32, 33, John Galt (Galt Collection, Museum of London) courtesy Ian Galt; p. 37 bottom, Dr Barnardo's; p. 80, Betty Fox, League of Jewish Women; p. 81 bottom, Joe Barnett; p. 82, Cheeper family; p. 92, David Jacobs, R. S. G. B.; pp. 104, 105, 107, 108, Donald Rumbelow and the City Police; p. 128, Radio Times Hulton Picture Library; pp. 34, 37 top, 58, 59, 61, Salvation Army; pp. 11 bottom, 24, 29, 30, 39, 51, 54, 60, 63, 65, 67, 79, 81 top, 109, 114, 116, 118, 119, 126, 127, 129, Tower Hamlets Public Library; frontispiece, pp. 6, 9, 10, 11, 12, 13, 14, 15, 16, 17, 18, 19, 20, 21, 22, 23, 25, 26, 27, 36, 41, 42, 43, 44, 45, 46, 47, 48, 49, 62, 69, 70, 71, 72, 73, 74, 75, 77, 78 right, 83, 84, 85, 86, 87, 89, 90, 91, 93, 94, 95, 96, 97, 98, 99, 100, 101, 102, 103, 111, 112, 113, 121, 122, 125, 130, 131, Nicholas Breach; pp. 135, 137, Ordnance Survey and the London Borough of Tower Hamlets.

Chanson...
Ne me Quitte Pas
Contra Na...
La Vie en Rose
Rien A Rien?
Come with Me
And they Die
Today el...
A Small Bird or Two

British
Ruskin
Morris
Bernard Shaw

Fr
Zola (realism)